SEVEN YEARS IN CEYLON

SEVEN YEARS IN CEYLON

Stories of Mission Life

BY

MARY AND MARGARET W. LEITCH

FOR ELEVEN YEAR MISSIONARIES OF THE AMERICAN BOARD OF COMISSIONERS FOR FOREIGN MISSIONS

WITH PORTRAITS AND MANY ILLUSTRATIONS

GYAN

Published by

Gyan Publishing House
5, Ansari Road
Daryaganj, New Delhi-110002
Phone: 011-47034999, 9811692060
E-mail: books@gyanbooks.com

Distribution Network
gyanbooks.com
India, USA, Canada, UK, Australia, France

ISBN : 978-81-212-4003-1 (PB)
First Published, 1890

2nd Impression 2020

Printed at: Gyan Press, Delhi.

SEVEN YEARS IN CEYLON.

A HINDU WOMAN

Seven Years in Ceylon

Stories of Mission Life

BY

MARY AND MARGARET W. LEITCH

FOR ELEVEN YEARS MISSIONARIES OF THE AMERICAN BOARD OF COMMISSIONERS FOR FOREIGN MISSIONS

WITH PORTRAITS AND MANY ILLUSTRATIONS

AMERICAN TRACT SOCIETY

150 NASSAU STREET, NEW YORK

TO

OUR TWO DEAR BROTHERS,

WHO, WITH UNFAILING KINDNESS,

HAVE CHEERED AND SUSTAINED US IN ALL WE HAVE ATTEMPTED TO DO

FOR THE FOREIGN FIELD,

We affectionately dedicate this book.

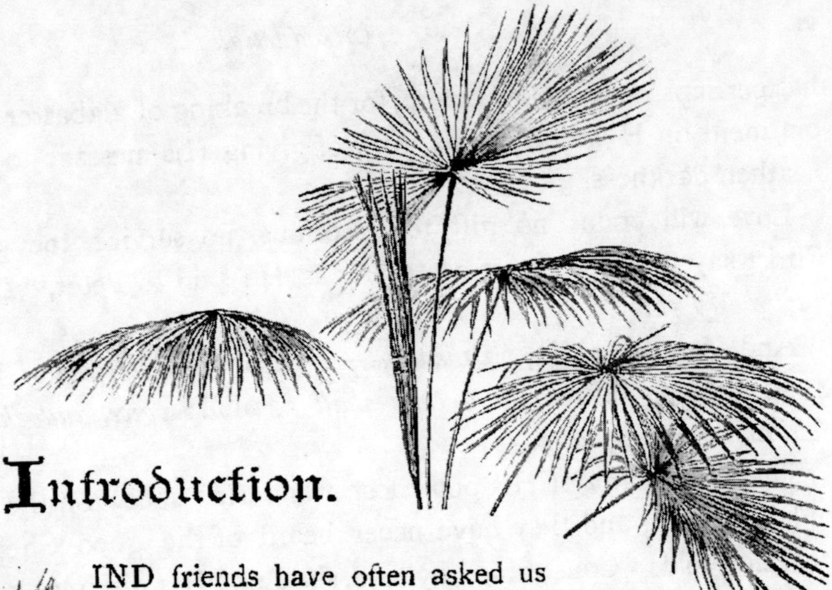

Introduction.

KIND friends have often asked us why, at the many meetings which we have addressed in behalf of the work of the Jaffna College in Ceylon, and the General Medical Mission about to be inaugurated in connection with it, we have not told more about the specific work in which we ourselves were engaged during the seven years which we spent in Ceylon as missionaries.

Our reply has been that, as we came to Great Britain with the special object of securing £30,000 for this College and Medical Mission, the time at our meetings has usually been consumed in presenting the claims of these special causes.

But while this was so, we have often wished that we had a compilation of some of the letters written from Ceylon at different times, giving our actual every-day experiences, to present to such kind friends.

Then again young ladies have often said to us, "Now please tell us about your own labours in Ceylon, and just what work we women can do in the foreign field." We have often felt an unspeakable longing, as we have looked into the bright, intelligent faces of the young ladies of this favoured land, that they might know more fully about the great opportunities of the present day for giving the Gospel to their sisters in heathendom. We believe that Christ is calling to the consecrated Christian young women of to-day, as He has perhaps never called before, for the breaking of alabaster boxes of precious ointment on His feet, in this work of giving His message to those who are in heathen darkness.

Love will count no gift too precious, no service too great. Does not Christ say to each one of us to-day as He said to Peter, "*Lovest thou Me?*" "*Feed My sheep.*"

And He says again, "*Other sheep I have which are not of this fold;* THEM ALSO I MUST BRING, *and they shall hear My voice, and there shall be one fold and one Shepherd.*"

There are many of His poor, lost, wandering sheep on the dark mountains of heathenism, and they have never heard of the good Shepherd or of the heavenly fold. Constrained by love, shall not His disciples go out after these lost ones with the prayer in their hearts, "*Let my* WHOLE LIFE *be a* SEARCH *for them*"?

MARY AND MARGARET W. LEITCH.

Table of Contents.

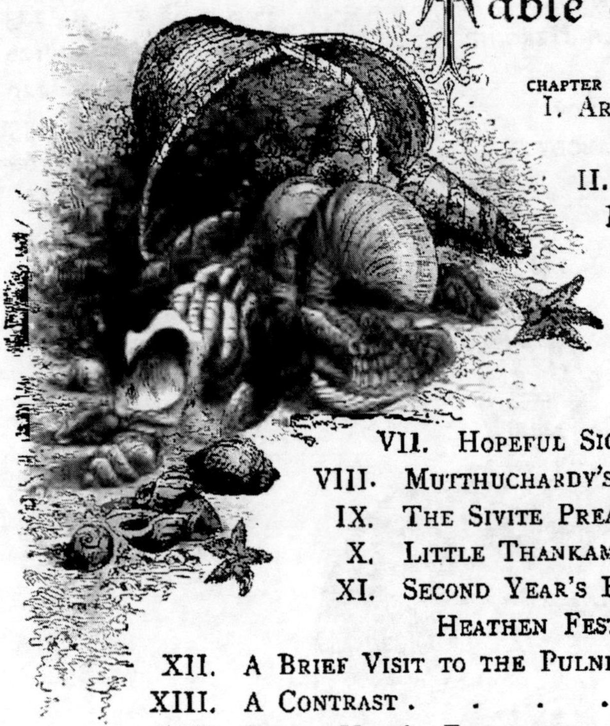

COLOMBO.

SEVEN YEARS IN CEYLON.

CHAPTER I.

Arrival and First Impressions in Ceylon.

Udupitty, Jaffna, Ceylon, *Feb. 6th*, 1880.

WE arrived here safely from Colombo on Jan. 14th. As we neared the shore of Jaffna we saw several handkerchiefs waved at us by missionaries who had come to meet us, and the words "Welcome home!" came over the water. We had supposed we were among strangers, but from that morning to this we have felt that we were at home with our friends. The bandies were waiting to take us to the mission-house at Udupitty, which is to be our home for the present. It seemed strange to be seated in a carriage before the horse had been attached; but we saw our mistake when six stout coolies (native runners) laid hold of the thills of the bandy and started off at a rattling pace, which they kept up nearly all the way. They passed over the sixteen miles between Jaffna town and Udupitty in a little over two and a half hours, preferring to go all the way themselves rather than be relieved by another set of coolies, because they wanted, as they said, to take the new missionaries home themselves.

When we were within a mile of the station, one of the coolies was despatched to herald our arrival. As we reached the mission premises we found the children of the station boys' school on one side and the station girls' school on the other, dressed in their best clothes, and the missionaries on the veranda steps ready to greet us. The veranda entrance-door and sitting-room had been adorned by the native Christians with festoons and wreaths of flowers, in honour of our coming. The native pastor and others were waiting to speak to us, and, in true Oriental fashion, the girls of the Udupitty Boarding-school, twenty-five in number, with their teachers, had prepared a lyric of welcome. Both words and tune were original with them, and they sang it very sweetly. We were deeply touched by this so unexpected and kind a reception. I translate the lyric here.

TAMIL GIRLS.

CHORUS.

"Come, let us sing—welcome!
Let us sing rejoicingly—joy! hurrah!"

SUB-CHORUS.

"Ye united members of the church,
The girls of the boarding-school,
Come," etc.

VERSES.

"May the new missionaries prosper.
They have come, with warm attachment,
To show the heavenly way to the multitudes of people, by pouring
In their ears the honey of the teachings of the Gospel. Joy! hurrah!
Come, let us sing—welcome, etc.

"That the knowledge may increase and the darkness be expelled,
And all sing hallelujah to the almighty Father,
The Son, and the Holy Ghost. Joy! hurrah!
Come, let us sing—welcome, etc.

"Praise the Lord for ever for the mercy of giving them
A safe arrival in Jaffna, passing over a long voyage. Joy! hurrah!
Come, let us sing—welcome," etc.

The second day after our arrival the annual business meeting of the mission was held at Udupitty. This gave us an opportunity to meet the other missionaries in the field. Among them were the Rev. and Mrs. W. W. Howland, who came out in 1846 and have grown old in this work. They have been called by some here a second Zacharias and Elisabeth, who walked in all the commandments and ordinances of the Lord blameless. There was also present Miss Eliza Agnew, the veteran missionary, who has been here forty years without going home, and who is a model of energy and decision. The magnitude of the work carried on here far exceeds our expectations. As we heard one report after another, reviewing the labours of the year, the schools supervised, the training of native catechists and teachers, the village work, the baptisms, and the communicants, the house visitations, tent meetings, etc., etc., we were filled with wonder, and could only praise the Lord and take courage, thanking Him that we were to be fellow-workers with such a band of noble men and women.

We are hard at work upon the language, with a native Munshee. Besides our regular lesson in the grammar and reader, we are learning some portions of Scripture and hymns. We can sing already, "Come to Jesus," "The Sweet By-and-By," and parts of other hymns in Tamil. We think in a week or two we shall pronounce with sufficient correctness to be able to join in the congregational singing.

THE HYMN "COME TO JESUS," IN TAMIL.	SOUND OF THE TAMIL WORDS IN ENGLISH.
யேசுவைச் சேர்.	Yea-su-vayt chare.
1. யேசுவைச் சேர்—இன்றே.	1. Yea-su-vayt chare—eun-day.
2. மீட்பார் உன்னை—இன்றே.	2. Meurd-pär une-ney—eun-day.
3. அன்பு கூர்வார்—இன்றே.	3. Än-pu koor-vär—eun-day.
4. நம்பி வாறேன்—இன்றே.	4. Num-pe vä-rane—eun-day.
5. அல்லேலூயா !—ஆமென்.	5. Al-le-lu-iah—ä-men.

The first Sabbath we were here, Mrs. Howland gave me the care of the infant Sunday-school class. They come from the chapel to my veranda, and all sit round me on a large mat, and look up with such bright, intelligent faces, that already I am beginning to love them very much. They number sixty little girls, all under ten years of age. Perhaps some people would laugh at me for calling them pretty, and say something about beauty unadorned; but though many of them wear only a single garment, yet their eager faces and attractive quiet ways make up for a good many deficiencies.

About forty native children come upon my veranda every afternoon to sew, and I talk to them, through an interpreter, and teach them Bible verses. My brother, sister, and I have gone out several times into the villages with the native helpers. The natives seem glad to see us, and ready to listen. Some of them say they do not believe in idols, and would become Christians if it were not that they would lose caste, and be persecuted by all their friends.

The missionaries of this station, the Rev. and Mrs. S. W. Howland and Miss Townsend, go out often in the morning and in the cool of the evening to hold meetings in the different villages. They have mothers' meetings at the mission-house, which are well attended by the heathen women. Sometimes they go out with the tent, remaining several days at a time in one place, and thus gain access to those who could not be reached in any other way. A few days ago they had the tent pitched at Thandemannar. In the afternoon the girls of this boarding-school went down in a body to sing, as the natives are very fond of music, and can often be moved by Christian songs. After they had sung several hymns, as there were a large number of heathen women and children present, Mrs. Howland suggested that each girl should take one or two women and talk with them for a little while. They received and acted upon the suggestion most beautifully, each girl sitting right down on the mats by the side of the one she was going to talk with, and one or two of the high-caste girls of the school gathering some of the little fisher-caste children around them. They talked very earnestly, and when, after a time, the missionary lady changed the order of exercises, they came to her, one after another.

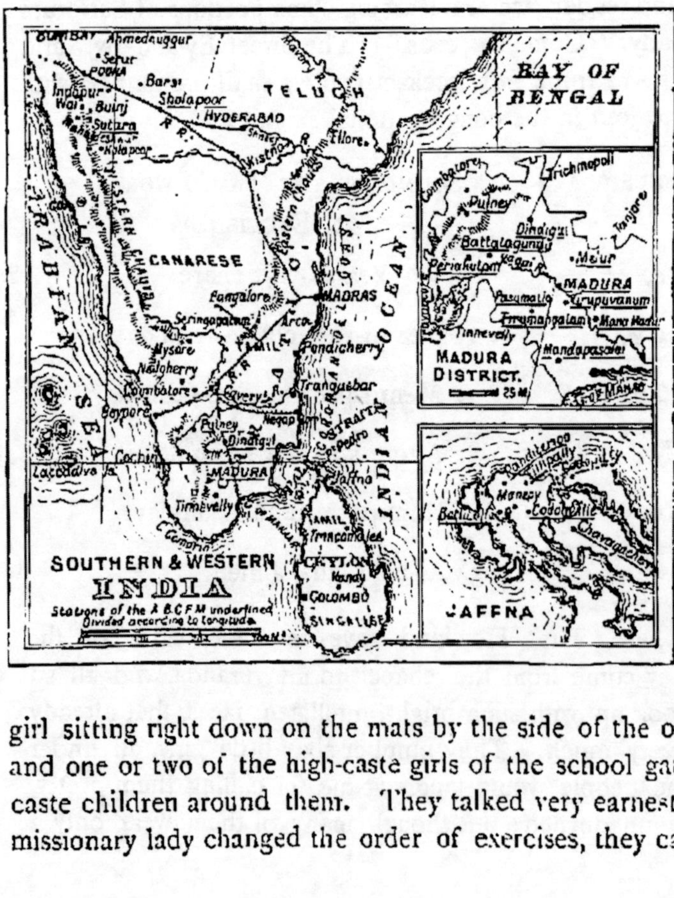

with such glowing faces, saying, "Oh, amma! I did have such a pleasant time with the little children!" or, "Oh, amma! the woman I was talking with promised to begin to pray to-night; and oh! won't we pray for her when we get home! Won't we all meet together and pray for these women!"

A few days after our arrival we had the pleasure of spending a day at Oodooville, seeing Miss Agnew and visiting the boarding-school. Here also they had prepared a lyric for us. We listened to five recitations, and we were all much pleased with the appearance of the school. New buildings are in process of erection, and the corner-stone is to be laid on February 10th. We also attended the annual examination and commencement exercises of Jaffna College. It was a most interesting occasion. All the examinations were in English, and considering that whatever the boys knew concerning the sciences, mathematics, philosophy and history, had been learned and must be repeated in a foreign tongue, the boys did great credit to their instructors.

I should like to tell you of the commencement exercises of the Udupitty Girls' Boarding-school, and of the monthly missionary meeting, where we met all the missionaries from the Wesleyan and Church Missionary Societies as well as our own, but I am writing too long a letter.

This is harvest-time, and the fields are full of reapers and gleaners. The work is all done by hand, the grain carried home on the heads of men and women, and threshed or trodden out by cattle. I am glad that our first impressions of the country should be received now, after the rainy season, when the island is covered with verdure, and looks fruitful and inviting.

I close with the following letter of greeting from Miss Agnew, which was given us soon after our arrival at Jaffna:—

MY DEAR MISSIONARY SISTERS:—With a warm heart and inexpressible delight do I give you Eliezer's welcome,—"Come in, thou blessed of the Lord."

For two years past have we sent the Macedonian cry, "Come over and help us." Though I was so anxious for two, yet my stinted faith would not allow me to revel in the anticipation that more than one would be added to our mission circle.

I do rejoice that our heavenly Father has sent you to this Eden of the East, and that you are allied in the ties of nature, and that you have a brother to aid and counsel you. This society may prevent loneliness from usurping even a small corner of your hearts. Every day prayer was offered for your safety while journeying on the sea and on the land.

You are coming to a goodly country, "where every prospect pleases"—no Anakims to fear. Your necessary weapons will be the living coals from the altar of the Lord in your hearts and upon your lips, and the sword of the Spirit in your right hands. Fear not: let timidity have no place: press forward; and in the spirit and with the language of the chief apostle to the Gentiles, say, in strong faith, "I can do all things through Christ which strengtheneth me." Necessity is laid upon every missionary to inscribe upon his breastplate, "Look unto Jesus," and to follow the example of the disciples of John the Baptist, who, after the burial, "went and told Jesus." The blood-bought mercy-seat will appear to you a more precious place in a heathen than in a Christian land. Deprived of so many of your spiritual aids, you will be more inclined to enter the holy of holies, where Jesus answers prayer.

I hope that you are as highly favoured as Heman's three daughters, who could sing in the house of the Lord. And though you may not understand how to strike the cymbal, or make melody on the harp, I trust you can handle the organ, and thus enhance the sweetness of our music whenever we frequent the gates of Zion.

I know of no other individual in any mission who has, like myself, remained at one station forty years. In relation to my work, in spirit I know no change, but physically I am weary, weary, weary, and need, as Jesus did, to "turn aside and rest awhile."

Yours, affectionately,

ELIZA AGNEW

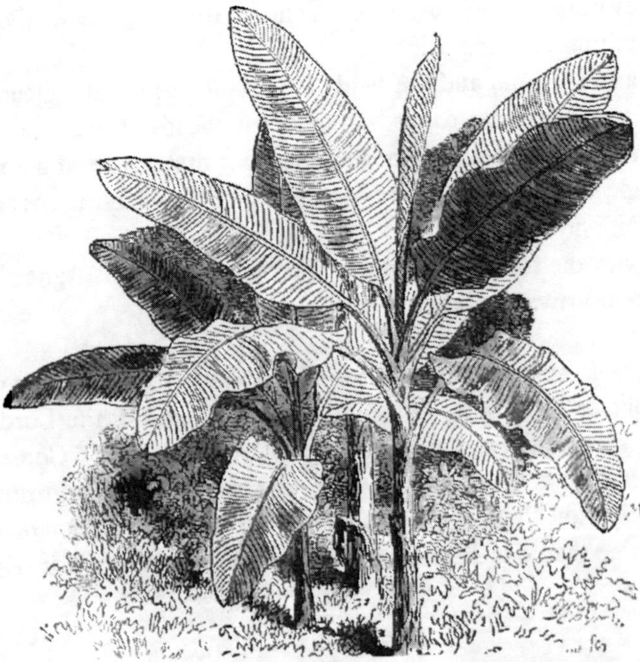

A CLUMP OF BAMBOOS.

CHAPTER II.

Revival Meetings.

Udupitty, *April 7th*, 1880.

WE left home last week, Tuesday, starting out in the early morning, and reached the Rev. and Mrs. T. S. Smith's, of Tillipally—having gone a distance of ten miles—in time for breakfast.

Can you imagine our ride that morning? The misty morning air was cool and invigorating. Our way lay through several villages. The road was level and well kept, and here and there shaded by beautiful clumps of bamboo, or by banyan, olive mango, margosa and other trees. The birds were singing merrily; the cocoanut and jack trees were laden with hanging fruit; and here and there a man might be seen climbing a smooth, tall palmyra palm. We studied Tamil all the way, while our coolies flew over the ground, needing no word from us except now and then a request not to go so fast. It is their pride to go fast, and they laugh and joke on the way, chaffing each other for going so slowly. When we reach our destination they usually eat their rice and curry, and then lie down on the ground to sleep in the shade of some tree, until we are ready to go on again. If we hold a meeting, they come in and listen.

From Tillipally we went to Oodooville. The special revival meetings commenced on Wednesday evening. Those who knew the people said that many came who had never been inside a church before. There were quite a number of requests for prayer sent in. They were given, in some instances, by people with tears running down their faces, so much in earnest were they that their friends might be brought to Christ. One man arose, his voice choked with emotion, and intimated that he had long been convinced of the truth of Christianity, and asked our prayers that he might become a Christian that day. One after another prayed for him, as they knew better than we his circumstances and the trials to which he would be exposed. It seems that he belongs to quite a good family, and his wife has a considerable property. Before he reached home the word had gone before him that he had asked for prayers, and his wife and family shut the door upon him, and drove him from the house. He has to sleep out of doors, and prepare his own food, while his friends either scoff and jeer at him, or refuse to notice him at all. We have just heard that he is standing firm, and that his younger son has joined him and wishes also to become a Christian. The elder son sides with the mother.

I notice by the American papers that during the month of March Jaffna was made a subject of prayer; so that while we were holding these meetings the people at home were bearing us up in their hearts before God. I have not the least doubt that those petitions were answered, for it was the opinion of all the missionaries present that the Spirit of God was wonderfully manifested. Native ministers and workers came from a distance of sixteen or eighteen miles, and they said they were going back to their people to hold special meetings among them. There were many working-women present, who were helping to erect the new school-building. They work as hard as men, from seven in the morning till six at night. But they attended the half-past six morning prayer-meeting, and went quietly out to work at seven, coming in again at seven in the evening and staying till nine; then they went into my sister's room, and listened eagerly while she talked and prayed with them. Nearly all expressed a desire

NEST OF THE TREE TERMITE (*Termes arborum*).

to become Christians, and some said they had begun to pray for themselves. They were so much in earnest that they did not seem to know that they were tired, and showed no inclination to leave, until my sister, quite worn out with the labours of the day—singing, playing on the organ, etc.—would tell them they might go.

Some of the women of a higher caste came into my room and prayed for one and another of their friends. Two came who had just decided to become Christians. One asked us to pray for her two daughters. "Oh!" she said, wringing her hands, "I have given them to heathen husbands, and if they are lost it will be my own work!" We tried to tell her that if she would strive for them, and pray in faith, God would hear her prayer. One woman prayed very earnestly that the Lord would make her duty plain. She said she loved Jesus Christ with her whole heart, and wanted to serve Him, but if she came out openly as a Christian her friends would discard her, and she was too old to earn her own living. What would she do in her old age? She would die of starvation. We could only pray that the Lord would guide her. I wish you could see how these people listen; how they lean forward to catch every word; how earnestly they pray. They seem hungry for the Bread of Life, and I am sure the Lord says, "They need not depart; give ye them to eat." When His disciples are ready to take the bread and give it to the people, and they are ready to give it to each other, all will soon be fed.

My sister and I had a meeting with the boarding-school girls at Oodooville, those who were Christians coming to my room, and those who were not to my sister's. The

Christian girls promised me that they would each take one or two of the non-Christian girls and pray specially for them till they became Christians. Those who were not told my sister, with tears in their eyes, that they wanted to become Christians that day; they were sorry to see the meetings close.

I have just received word from the Rev. Mr. Smith that four of the young men of the training-school, who attended the meetings, have decided to become Christians, and three from the Chunnargam boys' school. It is said that many men, especially those who have been educated in mission schools, would gladly become Christians, but are kept back by their heathen wives. These women, when not educated, are extremely bigoted. They tell their husbands that, if they become Christians, they will throw themselves into the well; and they mean what they say. These mothers take their young children to the temple and teach them to bow before the idol, and smear their faces with ashes. All this shows the importance of the education of girls in boarding-schools.

The people seemed to be more and more interested in the meetings each day. We hope to have another series of special meetings before long.

CHAPTER III.

Two Little Pariahs.

Udupitty, *June 1st*, 1880.

FOR several days, as I sat studying by my window, I noticed two bright little faces peering at me through the hedge. The new Ammas with their white skin and European dress are a great curiosity to the little brown-skinned children of this country. Some days after, my attention was attracted by a little coughing near my window. This is the way the Tamil people knock. When they wish to call upon us or among themselves, instead of knocking at the door as we would do, they stand outside and make a little noise, scraping with their feet, coughing, or sneezing. Looking up I saw the same two little faces which I had noticed before through the hedge.

PARIAH CHILDREN AT PLAY.

These two little boys were not dressed like children in America or England, but, like all little children here, wore only a strip of cloth about their loins. Their hair, which is generally allowed to grow long, was done up in a knot on the left side of the head over the left ear.

But their little graceful bodies, and their bright, eager faces, soon made one forget any peculiarities of colour or dress.

"Amma! Amma!" they said when I had called them to me, "we want to study reading at the boys' school." "Well," I said, "why do you not speak with the teacher about this?" "We cannot, we do not dare go into the yard, we are 'Pariahs,'" they said, as a pained look came into their eyes—a look sadly out of place in such young faces.

A CARPENTER.

The system of caste runs through the whole fabric of society here. In each caste the descendants must follow the occupation of their parents. If a man is a carpenter, for example, his sons must all become carpenters, and his daughters must marry carpenters. The different castes have no opportunity to rise, but are doomed to remain in the condition in which they are born. They do not intermarry, do not mingle together socially, do not eat together, but are essentially different communities of people.

There is the highest, or Brahmin caste, who are priests—thick, fat fellows, who never do any work; then the farmers, their servants, carpenters, blacksmiths, goldsmiths and their washers; and next the tree-climbers and their washermen; and lastly the weavers, drum-beaters and their washermen. Each keep to their own work, and each are heartily despised by the caste above them, and in the same way look down upon the caste below them. Even the drum-beaters' castes have a caste under them to do their washing. It was to this, the "Pariah Caste," these two little boys who stood by my window said they belonged. A century ago, in the darker days of Ceylon, this caste of people were never allowed to leave their houses except in the night, and then they were obliged to drag a large branch behind them, so that any one of a higher caste walking in the street might hear and call upon them to turn aside until they had passed; for to touch, speak to, or even look at a person of this low caste was considered a pollution.

What a disgrace to put upon a human being made in the image of God! Shame on the religion of Siva which upholds and fosters such wickedness. Under English rule the Pariahs have liberty to go and come as they please; but they are everywhere scorned and oppressed.

They have some queer customs. Often poor tree-climbers own only a single cloth. In order to wash this they ask the washerman, and he does not refuse, to lend them the cloth of some other person which he has taken to wash, while he takes and washes theirs; thus it is not an uncommon thing for one to see his cloth, which he has sent to be washed, worn on the person of a stranger. The washerman stands knee-deep in water and bleaches the garments by knocking them over the stones, swinging them over his head as a thresher does his flail; to dry them he spreads them by the road-side on the hot sand, and places a few stones on the corners to keep them from blowing away. He is rarely paid in money, but is generally given the leavings of table food and a little rice and curry stuffs.

We told the two little boys, whose names we learned were Kassappu and Kadpeyal, that if they would come the following day, with their bodies bathed and their hair nicely combed, we would go with them our-

WASHERMEN.

selves to the school. The first thing which I saw on looking out of my window early the next morning was the two little boys watching for me. I went with them to the school, but could hardly induce the little fellows to enter; they fairly trembled with fear as they stood in the presence of higher caste boys. After years of persistent effort, the missionaries have succeeded in inducing the children of a large number of castes to study together in the schools, though it is amusing to see the highest caste boys sometimes bringing little mats with them on which to sit, and so preserve their tottering dignity. The teacher, a Christian native, willingly promised to receive and do his best for the little boys. We passed through the school bungalow with its thatched roof, where the higher standards were studying, through the veranda where the middle standards were reciting, and came into the yard, where, under the trees, sat twenty or more little boys busily engaged writing out their lessons with little sticks in the sand.

I motioned Kassappu and Kadpeyal to sit down with the others, when lo! as quick as lightning, these twenty little naked morsels of society scattered on all sides as if they had been poisoned, crying, "Cha! Cha!" while one gave the youngest little boy a vicious pinch, and another actually spat at them. How strange that children five and six years old could imbibe and cherish such bitter prejudices!

The two little boys sat that day in a corner of the yard by themselves, but the next day brought word that the whole school was threatening to leave, and even the Maniagar or head man of the village had sent word that, if these low-caste boys came, he would not allow his child to come. I decided that rather than break up the school I would for the present teach the boys myself. This storm of public sentiment was a great surprise to me. The upper caste said, "If this caste be educated, who will do our washing?"—the old spirit of slavery which has only lately been wiped out in our own land.

The little boys came to our veranda each day for a lesson, and learned well, mastering the 247 letters of the Tamil alphabet with surprising quickness. They learned many things outside of their books, among others to say "Good morning," and "Thank you." One day we showed them a picture-book. They had never seen a picture before in all their lives, poor things, but when I pointed out to them the children and trees and animals in the pictures, they caught at the idea. You should have seen their delight, and have heard their shout when they themselves discovered a cat and a dog.

One day, while they were with us, a class of fourteen large boys, whose Bible lesson in English my sister had kindly offered to teach through the term, came in. When they saw these two poor little washer-boys they fairly glared at them. Sister said, "Why do you look so angry?" They answered, "Those boys have no right to come here. They are low caste. If we should take up a little stick they would run from us. It is not the custom of the country to show them any attention." That is the excuse here for every kind of evil practice. "It is the custom of the country, ma'am." Sister went up to the little boys, and putting her hand on the head of the older, said, "God made this little boy as well as you. He gave to him an immortal soul as well as to you. Jesus Christ died to save him and you. You will both stand together in the judgment. God says He hates pride, and if you are proud and despise this little boy for whom Jesus Christ died, you sin against God."

The next day the school boys did not come, and the reason given was that my sister had disgraced herself by touching these boys of a low caste, and they did not wish to be taught by such a person. We said nothing, knowing that the class enjoyed coming too well to deprive themselves of it long. And we were right. They came the following morning with a shamefaced look.

Kassappu and Kadpeyal continue to come to us, and are just the brightest, funniest, most affectionate little boys I ever saw. They are philanthropic little fellows too; for finding themselves well received, and expanding under kindness like flowers in the sunshine, they came bringing three other little boys and two little girls, who they insist, with all earnestness, must also learn to read.

What a shame that all their caste, from no fault of their own, should practically be shut out from social privileges, and condemned to be always poor, ignorant, and despised, with no bright future before them in this life, and with no prospect in view for the life to come, according to Hinduism, but to live again on earth, perhaps as an insect or a snake!

In contrast with all this how should we thank God for giving to the world His dear Son, a Saviour to the poor and the lost! The sight which I saw a few days ago, of three hundred Christian natives sitting down without regard to caste at the common table of our Lord, gave proof of what the Gospel has done, and a promise of what it will do yet more abundantly in this land.

As sure as God's word is true, so surely may we rely on the promise, "The whole earth shall be filled with the knowledge of the glory of God."

MANEPY MISSION HOUSE AND PUPILS FROM THE STATION SCHOOLS.

CHAPTER IV.

First Year's Review.

Manepy, *December 16th*, 1880.

TIME has flown so swiftly of late that I cannot realize that it is a year and three months since we left America, nearly a year since we landed in Jaffna, and ten weeks since we came to Manepy. This year has been the busiest, and I think, all things considered, the happiest year of my life. I can truly say that I have never for one moment regretted my coming to Ceylon, but have felt thankful to God for permitting me to be a co-labourer with the missionaries in this land.

As you may know, there are over 300,000 people in North Ceylon. Labouring among them are two families under the English Church Mission, two under the English Wesleyan Mission, and five under our own; which allows an average of over 30,000 people to each missionary family. What would any pastor at home think of such a charge?

Manepy is one of the smaller stations, and we have within its boundaries only about 10,000 people.[1] There are two Christian churches—one here at the station, the other at Navaly—numbering together one hundred and four communicants. There is one pastor, and another to be ordained very soon. As helpers, there are

1 A short time after this the station of Panditerippu also was given into our care.

two catechists and two Bible-women. These do much faithful house-to-house work in the villages, hold cottage meetings and Sabbath services, and assist in our large tent-meetings. The church-members, as a whole, are active and earnest. They have surprised us by their willingness to co-operate with us and act upon our suggestions. As far as I have means of knowing them personally, I am led to think that they are truly God's children, really changed by the Holy Spirit. The missionary work would not have been a failure here had it done nothing more than save and bless these men and women.

We have within the Manepy district eight Sabbath-schools, with thirty-four teachers, and an average attendance of eight hundred scholars. Three of these have been organized during the last two months, and all have increased in their attendance. The station Sabbath-school has increased from not quite one hundred to two hundred and thirty-five, and will, I hope, number three hundred before New Year's Day. If you could look in upon us with our eighteen teachers and classes nicely graded, our "International Lesson Leaves," and Sankey's hymns in Tamil, our organ and blackboard, you would forget for the moment, I think, that you were in a heathen land.

There are in the Manepy district ten day-schools, supported mainly by Government grants, but under the direction of a Board of Education, composed of native Christians and missionaries. In these schools are thirty-one teachers, the majority of whom are Christians. This is an important field, and we hope to make the most of it. The teachers, both Christian and heathen, were delighted with our proposition to visit the schools once a week and devote an hour in each to the study of a Bible lesson. We sold several hundred copies of the Gospel of Matthew in Tamil, selected a verse of scripture to be learned and a portion to be read each day, secured the co-operation of the teachers in teaching the lesson every day during the first hour in the morning, and mapped out the schools for our weekly round of visits.

The plan has succeeded thus far beyond our highest expectations. The teachers have entered heartily into it, for they feel that our weekly visits will prove a real encouragement to the schools and an honour to themselves, so highly are the missionaries esteemed throughout Jaffna. The moment we are seen approaching the school, all lay aside their books, and when we enter they rise and give us salaams. The seats have been already arranged, and we take our different classes and go over the different lessons of the week, which have been so well prepared that only once have we had reason to complain. We try to make the lessons enjoyable, and slowly, but surely, we hope to win our way into the confidence of the children, and make them our friends. The aim of all our efforts is to win them to Jesus Christ.

Sixteen young men are studying in a select school at the station. As they come from heathen homes, they find, after having lived under Christian influence for some time, that their old faith is shaken, and their minds are full of doubts. To meet these doubts we asked them to write out any points that were troubling them, or questions they would like to ask, and we promised on each Monday afternoon to answer them, as far as we could. Since then the questions have poured in upon us, and the eagerness with which they lean forward and listen to our answers, and the remarks they make in return, show that the difficulties are real, and their minds alive and active.

I will give you a few specimens of their questions: "What is religion?" "What is the cause of the existence of the different religions?" "What are the evidences that the Christian religion is true?" "What are the external evidences that Christ, rather than Mahomet and Buddha, was a revelation of God?" "If Christ paid the penalty for our sins, why did He not suffer to all eternity?" "Why did God place the forbidden fruit in the garden, when He knew Adam would disobey?" "Why was Jacob blessed instead of Esau?" "Why did the angels fall from heaven—is it a place of temptation?" "What will become of the soul between death and the judgment?" "If the doctrine of transmigration is not true, why are men born blind or deformed, if not for some former sin?" etc.

Since they themselves ask these questions, we have an opportunity to tell them some truths from which they cannot get away, and which are destined to stay in their minds until they are either answered or accepted. We have had their cheerful assent, thus far, to all we have said. We have allowed them perfect freedom of speech, and have endeavoured never to leave a point until it was fully understood. Our hearts yearn over these sixteen young men in their opening manhood. Will you not pray with us that they may truly find the light of life?

We have a meeting for native Christian mothers and children on Tuesday afternoons, which usually numbers fifty or sixty. The Christian women lead in prayer, repeat verses, and take turns in leading the meeting and explaining the Scripture lesson. Our great desire and hope for Manepy is, that every Christian woman may take it up as her work to teach some three or four heathen women to read the Bible. This would be a permanent influence, reaching out into the heathen homes, and, step by step, the heathen mothers might be led to pray to God, to come to church, and, finally, to Jesus. The seclusive and exclusive habits of Eastern women, together with caste distinctions and their strong prejudices, make it very difficult to carry out this plan; still, "with God all things are possible." The women have already made a beginning, and twelve pupils were reported at our last meeting, besides those whom the Bible-women reach regularly.

In the moonlight evenings, through half of the month, we have tent meetings, which are quite largely attended. We have a good-sized tent, received from Madras, which our coolies can put up in forty-five minutes, and take down in fifteen. If we go out with the tent, organ, lamps, hymn-books, etc., we are sure to have a good audience in almost any village. We have had from one hundred and fifty to two hundred at these gatherings.

The rainy season is upon us now, which makes it a little difficult to get about through the muddy fields and lanes. The rice-fields are flooded, but our coolies are always ready to take us anywhere and in any weather. These coolies are really a great comfort, and are useful in many ways besides drawing the bandy. They have begun to learn to read, and are making good progress. It is interesting when we are in the schools to see them sitting outside, studying their books in the interval of waiting. The three whom we employ regularly have learned the Lord's Prayer in Tamil, and their voices join with ours every morning as we repeat it at the close of family prayers. They go to church and Sabbath-school. It is our prayer that they may soon truly know our Saviour, and give their hearts to Him. They seem quite like friends to us now, and we are so accustomed to them that we do not notice, as we did at first, their dark skins, shaven heads, or the absence of all clothing except a yard or two about the waist. They cannot be induced to wear more, both on account of the heat and because it is not the custom among their caste. Their only food is rice and curry, which they cook themselves. Their whole expense amounts to about $2.25 in American money per month for each.

Our home in Manepy is a very pleasant one. The compound is large, and has over forty kinds of trees. Near the house we have the flambo, now just ready to burst into a glory of scarlet blossoms; the cork-tree, with its white clusters of sweet-smelling flowers, which cover the ground like snow; and on the other side the tamarind, with its acid fruit-pods. There are mahogany, olive, margosa, teak, iron-wood, ebony, mango, jack, wood-apple, and many other kinds of trees in the yard. Above them shoot up the cocoa-nut and Palmyra palms, with their magnificent tall trunks and great tufted heads.

Our house has three large and four small rooms, all on the ground floor, which is raised about four feet above the ground. The walls are of stone and mortar; the floors are of the same, to prevent the invasion of white ants. We have only a few glass windows; the other windows, as well as the doors, are supplied with shutters, which may be used at night to give security, and a free access of air at the same time.

THE JACK TREE, SHOWING FRUIT.

Our furniture is the plain, cane-bottomed kind; some of it brought from America, the rest made here by native carpenters, who imitate English patterns with great exactness. We have learned to like rice and curry, and nearly all the native fruits and products. Our dress for the whole year is of white material, plainly made.

Our flower-garden in front of the house provides our table with fresh roses daily; and our vegetable garden contains over forty plantain-trees. There is nothing dreary about the rainy season; it seems to us the pleasantest part of the year. Everywhere the new grass is very green and fresh, and the sun shines out brightly after the heavy showers. The mercury stands at about 85° in the shade without much change. In the house in the hottest season the mercury seldom rises above 93°, and rarely falls in the coolest season below 76°.

SHRINE OF THE GOD PULLIAR.

CHAPTER V.

A Visit to a Heathen School.

Manepy, *March 11th*, 1881.

JUDGING by what we can learn from the experience of the missionaries who have been here longest, it would seem that the work among the young is followed by the most encouraging results.

We visit our schools every week, giving a Bible-lesson. Many of the children can now repeat the Lord's Prayer, the Ten Commandments, and the greater part of the fifth and sixth chapters of Matthew; they are at present learning the seventh. Some have committed to memory the twenty-third and one-hundred-and-third Psalms. We take our little organ with us, as they have learned many of the Sankey hymns, and many Christian lyrics. I rejoice to think, when these boys and girls shall have grown to be men and women, how very precious these hymns will become to them.

Our great desire is to get all these children into the Sabbath-school, and we are trying to enlist the teachers on our side. In one school, we have succeeded better than we wished. Only last week we discovered that the teacher was in the habit of calling up the scholars every Monday morning to ask if they had attended Sabbath-school the day before, and if they had not, they would receive a whipping! When we asked for an explanation, we were told that they had tried the plan of giving a good mark to those who had attended, and a bad one to those who had not; but as some of the scholars were always at the foot of the class, this had no effect upon them, and so they thought they would try something else. Of course, we explained that however effective this might be in one direction, it utterly failed in accomplishing our main object, which was to win the love and sympathy of the children for the Sabbath-school; and that we would try to make the place so attractive that they would want to come.

In one school, a private school not connected with our mission, situated in Santilipay, which is the strongest Sivite community in this field, we have not yet obtained a permit to teach. We visited the school, a short time ago, with a permission, or rather with an invitation, from the manager to do so. A relative of one of the teachers volunteered to accompany us; but it seems that the teachers, knowing that we were coming, had determined that Christianity should be kept out of their school. When we entered three of the teachers received us courteously, but the fourth seemed more opposed to Christianity than the others. After we had listened for awhile to various recitations we asked:—

"Is English taught in this school?"

"Why should we teach English?" he asked. "It is not a primitive language. Sanscrit is the primitive language."

"Don't you think there are many valuable books in English?"

"The most valuable books are in Tamil," he answered. "The books in English are not true. The works of the greatest writers who have ever lived are in Sanscrit."

"You are an educated man," we replied, "and you know that the most valuable books in science—those which you accept and believe—are found not in the Tamil or the Sanscrit, but in the English."

"What do we care for science?" he asked in reply. "Our religious books are in Sanscrit."

"Well, this is not a matter on which we need to dispute," we said. "You have studied English, and we are learning Tamil."

At this point one of the teachers said, "We have a class in English, and we would like to have you examine it, if you please." So he called up a class, and my brother examined them in their studies, commended them a little, and interested them in some subjects of which they had not thought before.

As we had been visiting other schools in the morning, we had our little organ with us, and had let our coolies carry it into this school-room. We noticed that the organ had been regarded with considerable curiosity, and we asked if they would like to have us sing something. "Nothing religious," said the teacher before spoken of; but the others all said, "Yes, yes; please sing something." So we sang, "There's a land that is fairer than day," in Tamil. The children were delighted, and at once gathered around as close as they could get to us. When we had sung a little we proposed to go, not wishing to infringe upon their time. We said to the teachers that it would give us pleasure to have them call on us, when they felt disposed to do so.

When coming away we noticed that the teacher whom we had talked with had trouble with his eyes, and on inquiry we were surprised to learn that he was totally blind. The moment we showed interest in his eyes his manner changed, and his anxiety was very great as we examined the eyes. Oh, what would he not give for sight! We told him that possibly his sight might be restored; but he did not know that it could be, as he has been doctoring with native drugs. We asked him to come to our house, and we would note down his symptoms; and he consented with great eagerness. He came a little time afterward, and we had considerable conversation with him. If his sight could be restored by going to Madras for an operation, it would be a great event in favour of Christianity in the region where he lives.

The same day that we visited the Sivite school, we had a moonlight meeting in the village. We felt some anxiety with regard to it, as there were so many educated

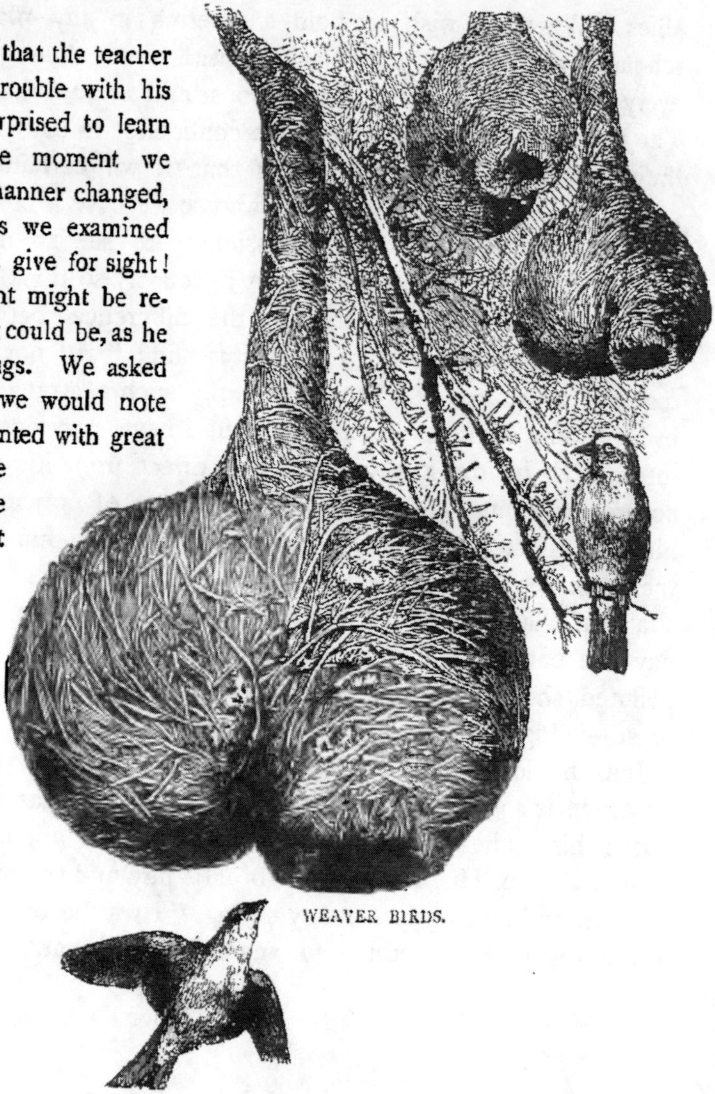

WEAVER BIRDS.

people in the place who were strong Sivites. We noticed, also, that the Christians looked troubled, and they told us afterwards that several heathen had come—as they said—to break up the meeting; but as He arranged it who cares even for the sparrows, who numbers the hairs on our heads, and who holds the hearts of all men in His hands, we were not molested. Fortunately there was a Christian man of high caste with us, who had considerable influence over the people. As my sister and I spoke, it was something so new to hear ladies speak that they listened not only with attention, but seemed to lean forward to catch every word. They even paid us the compliment of saying to one of the Christians that we were "very clever speakers;" meaning, I suppose, very clever for women.

We have tried to win the confidence of the children, and they are proving our best allies. When we wish to hold a meeting in any place we have only to tell the scholars, and they come, and bring with them their parents and friends. Almost every day the children come to our house and ask, "Where is the next meeting to be?" The little things seem to have much confidence in us; if any of their friends are sick they come to us at once, expecting that we will certainly come and visit them. We cannot disappoint their faith in us, and so we have a busy life.

It is one of the trials of a missionary to see so much sickness and poverty as I suppose there must always be in a country so thickly populated as this. People at home can hardly appreciate the difference between the higher and lower castes of this country. "What!" it is said; "will not the people in India even sit together in church?" But is it really such a strange thing? I have worshipped in handsome churches in America, but I never saw one of the elegant members lead into church by the arm an Irishman direct from his work on the streets—his feet covered with mud, and his clothing guiltless of contact with soap and water—show him into his seat, and share his hymn-book with him. But the difference between these two people would not represent that between a Brahmin and a Pariah. The Brahmin is fastidiously clean; it is a part of his religion. His clothing is washed every day; he bathes before every meal; the things by which he would consider himself polluted, should they touch him, are almost innumerable. His mind—in a certain sense—is highly cultured.

But the low caste—God pity him!—how hard a lot is his! His struggle for existence is so great that his spirit is broken; he has no courage. He very seldom washes his clothes—at least so I judge from their appearance. I speak to him of the love of God, of His fatherly care, of His pity and sorrow for us, of Jesus Christ as his Saviour, and he surprises me by saying, "I will become a Christian if you will tell me where I will get something for my children to eat." I begin to think that he who

A PREACHING SERVICE.

could make two spears of paddy grow where only one grows now would be a benefactor indeed. There is not a plough in this province. They still use a crooked stick, which only scratches the surface of the ground; and when a drought comes everything is burnt up, and we have a famine. I am mistaken; there is one plough here, but it is too heavy for use.

I am sure that the great poverty of many is a hindrance to their becoming Christians. We are trying to fight against the spirit of caste. We are endeavouring to teach the higher castes to pity and help the lower castes, and treat them as their brethren in Christ. We have succeeded in getting a good many of the low-caste women and children, and some men, to attend the church and Sabbath-school. We tried to have them sit on the benches. We said, "When we come into God's house let there be no difference." But the lower castes would not sit on the benches; they are not accustomed to it: they have not such a thing as a chair in their small houses. They sit on a mat spread on the ground, and if we should insist on their sitting on seats, they would not come to church; so we have spread nice clean mats on the right and left side of the pulpit, and they are very happy sitting there.

Our Christians, who are mostly of high-caste, strive very hard to help the lower classes. I hardly know of a Christian woman in Manepy who has not pledged herself to give a part of one day each week to go out into the villages to teach and help those poor people. They do this although some of them have large families, and hard work to do at home.

My letter has grown long, and yet it seems to me that I have scarcely spoken about our work. I will simply say that we love it; that we feel strong and well, to do it; and that we like the field at Manepy very much.

A HINDU TEMPLE.

CHAPTER VI.

A Great Heathen Festival.

Manepy, *May 1st*, 1881.

THE great annual heathen festival of the temple here, lasting twelve days, began the 1st of April. This temple, which is now one of the most celebrated in Jaffna, was forty years ago only a little hut at the base of a large tree, and was supposed to be inhabited by the god Pulliar. Superstitious and ignorant people vowed, in times of sickness, to make offerings to this god if he would cure them. Gifts began to pour in; the story of imagined cures spread; and thus in forty years a large and richly endowed temple has grown up, to which thousands of devotees flock yearly from all the surrounding country. Perhaps the fact that it was just opposite our Christian church and mission premises helped its growth, for many Sivites gave toward it for the purpose of showing their opposition to Christianity. It is one of eight large temples in this peninsula, besides which there are five hundred smaller ones, each with priests and daily offerings, not to mention the thousands of family shrines and household gods.

The daily exercises of the twelve days' feast are as follows: At six o'clock every morning the bell is rung, and people gather at the temple. The stone idol of Pulliar is in the innermost court; it represents the god as having an elephant's head, four arms, large abdomen, and two dwarf legs, on which he sits Turkish-fashion. The idol, bathed carefully with milk and perfumes, is then clothed and decorated with jewels, and his forehead marked with the sacred ashes, and the third eye of Siva. The veil is then opened, and fruits, rice, etc., brought by the worshippers, are offered before him. Incense is burned; prayers unintelligible to the people are uttered by the priests; and songs to his praises, instrumental music, &c., complete the ceremony.

Some sacred ashes and pounded sandal-wood offered to the god are passed to the worshippers, who mark themselves on forehead, neck, arms, breast and back with the stripes of Siva. As these things are offeied first to the highest caste, and thence downward, many quarrels arise as to which families are the highest in rank. The priest gives each one a flower, which is placed behind the ear or in the coil of hair. The same process is next gone through to a flagstaff, standing in the middle of the courtyard; and thirdly to a small brass image of Pulliar. Every morning or evening some of the more devout, wishing to atone for sin or to perform a work of merit, roll on their almost naked bodies around the temple, over the earth and stones; the women, bowing and touching their hands on the ground, wipe their faces in the dust, rise and place their feet where the head touched before, fall forward again, and so measure their length around the temple.

During the festival the ceremonies are repeated at noon, and the brass idol is taken out for a ride around the court of the temple. He is carefully fastened on the back of a large painted wooden rat or peacock, or some other animal—each day a different one—which is borne on the shoulders of men. At night—beginning at midnight and lasting till two o'clock in the morning—with torchlight and music, the god is given his ride around the outside of the temple. For twelve nights our rest has been entirely broken by the deafening horns, drums, and cymbals, mingled with the shouts of the people and the explosion of various kinds of fireworks. All through these midnight festivals a troop of dancing-girls of the most abandoned character dance before the idol and the populace.

The twelfth and last day of the feast was the great car-drawing day. By eight o'clock in the morning people on foot or in ox or horse-bandies began pouring in from all sides, until the lanes, roads and broad rice-fields on two sides of the temple swarmed with more than ten thousand people. The air grew blue with the smoke of hundreds of fires, where on every hand food was being cooked in the open air for the idol. Only the steam or odour is acceptable to the god, so the cooked rice is carried home, or given to the priests or to mendicants, which is considered a work of merit. The low caste people cannot be allowed even to enter the court of the temple and make their own offerings; some high-caste person must carry the food in and present it for them, bringing it back afterwards to the donor. To the large temple-tank hundreds of people go to drink the muddy, stagnant holy waters; wash away their sins by bathing their bodies; and wash their clothes preparatory to making their offerings. In the same tank the heated oxen stand, cooling their bodies and being washed by their owners.

After a time the cavadies began to arrive. These are fantastic wooden frames decked with flowers, peacock-feathers and tinsel, carried on the head and shoulders

HINDUS BATHING.

of the individual from his house to the temple, in performance of a vow in time of sickness. The bearer prepares for the ceremony by some days of fasting. He is accompanied by a band of music, and comes whirling and dancing as if possessed with a spirit. The people suppose him to be filled with the spirit of the god, and so to be specially holy; but alas for the holiness of which this is a type! A year ago a quarrel took place between a cavady bearer from Batticotta and one from Anikotty; and it was rumoured that the quarrel would be renewed this year. In the middle of the festival shouts were heard, and thousands upon thousands of people left the temple and the idols and rushed to the scene of action. It was a stampede such as I have never before witnessed. Instantly, as it seemed, four hundred or more Batticotta men, seizing sticks from the nearest fences, began to assault about half as many Anikotty men, and before they could be separated several were severely wounded. These were brought bleeding to our dispensary, and my brother and a native Christian physician were left to undo the work which heathen passion had done. In the case of one poor man it was all in vain; he died the next day. We have used this as a warning and a sermon in many of our talks with the young people, who admit at once that going to the temples and washing in sacred waters do not make the heart holy. The older heathen, however, do not seem troubled by what was done, but hope that the excitement will be twice as great next year. It is not strange that those who worship such cruel gods and goddesses should in a measure become like them.

To return to the car-drawing: The huge old car on cumbrous wheels had been decorated with flowers and flags and cloth; the small brass idol was placed within, and many Brahmans attended, to burn incense before it. Eighty men or more seized hold of the two thick ropes, and thus it was drawn around the temple, followed by rolling devotees. When half-way round it paused before a pile of a thousand cocoa-nuts, which one man had vowed to break with his right hand before the idol by throwing them one after another on a stone. This finished, the car returned to its place, and the people began to disperse.

But what were our Christians doing during all this time? Over thirty of the leading Christian workers from this and the neighbouring stations, by our invitation, met together at our house in the morning, and after a season of earnest prayer for God's help and blessing, they took bundles of tracts, handbills and books, and went out in various directions on the different roads and lanes leading from the temple, in order to meet and talk with the people on their return, and sell or give away tracts and books. Then we, with five prominent native Christians, took our stand on the veranda of the medical-room, which is just across the way from the temple, and where mats and benches had been arranged. We opened all the stops of our organ, and began singing praise to Christ in a strong, full chorus. Soon a crowd of from three to four hundred people gathered around us. Our method was to explain a verse of a lyric, and then sing; then another verse and sing, and so on. We kept this up for four hours, a large and interested crowd being by us all the time. We noticed in our audience Brahmans, Sivite preachers, and the editor of a Sivite paper; all listened respectfully without a particle of disturbance, and some faces here and there showed marked interest. Our book-stand near by was doing a good business in selling tracts and portions of the Bible; and word came back from several companies that they had nearly sold out their tracts, and that more were wanted.

Our workers were thoroughly aroused, and spoke and sang their very best. One good Christian from a neighbouring church, who had said in the morning that he did not think it was of much use to try this kind of work—the festival had gone on for a long time, and not much if anything had ever been done about it—now, talking to his audience, became so interested that he refused the offer of lunch; and at night went away declaring that this was just the way to do, and that next year many Christians from all the stations must come, and we would have meetings on five or six sides. The Christians returned encouraged, and we could see that the effort had done them good, if no one else. All seemed surprised at the readiness with which the people bought religious books and tracts; and many were seen reading them in companies under trees and in their bandies, on their way home. In all, *during this one day, two thousand nine hundred and fourteen tracts, small books, and portions of Scripture were sold by us and our helpers, and three thousand six hundred and eighteen were given away.*

May the seed sown by the wayside, with God's blessing, spring up and bring forth fruit to His glory!

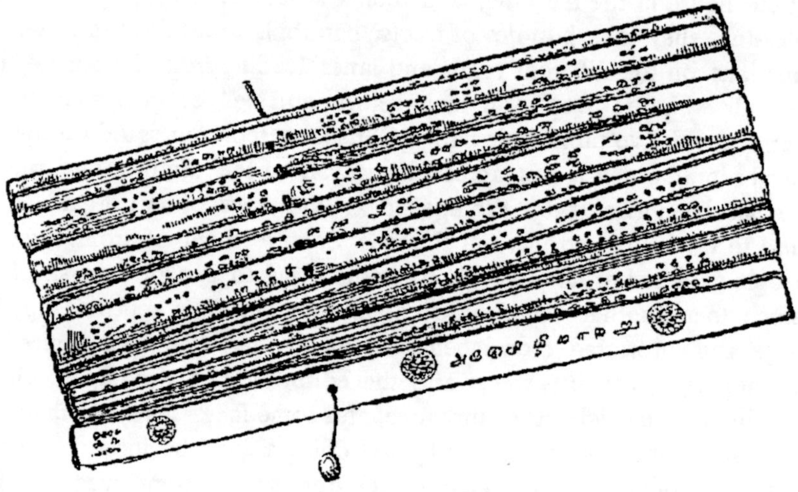

A TAMIL "BOOK."

CHAPTER VII.

Hopeful Signs.

Manepy, *October 31st*, 1881.

WHILE we long and pray and hope that God's Spirit may be poured out among us in an unusual manner, yet it seems more probable that the blessing will come quietly through the widespread and faithful teaching of the truth, and the inclining of more and more hearts to accept it. I confess that I find myself greatly perplexed to understand the mental processes of, for example, our older English-speaking school-boys. For a year, in day-school, Sabbath-school, and in private talks, they have heard the truth, and have understood it. They can tell the story of Christ's life nearly as well as I can. They have had the nature of prayer, the duty of faith and repentance, clearly explained.

Why then do they not become Christians? They have not yet given up their old beliefs. These beliefs are ingrained into their literature, their history, their song, their every-day duty and thought. They say that, although we are right, there is much that is right with them also. They are bound to their friends by the strongest ties, and the fetters are riveted by caste. It is a terrible wrench to break away from all.

All these things, and many more, bear on the probable future. Yet of one thing we are sure, that the steady, faithful, earnest teaching of God's own word in church

HINDUS WORSHIPPING AN IDOL.

and school, in public and private, must be followed by a steady growth of conscientiousness and love for truth throughout the community, and by a larger and larger number of individuals turning to God. The Gospel has all along in the past been moulding this whole community.

Is it nothing that we have almost the whole educational work in our hands, that nearly every house is open to our visits and those of the catechists and Bible-women; that the attendance at church and Sabbath-school is increasing; that moonlight, village, and Sabbath afternoon meetings are so largely attended? All the educated men and women, and the older children in the schools, are ashamed of the ceremonies connected with the Sivite worship and the great festivals, and do not participate in them. All through the villages there are men and women who do not rub ashes or visit heathen temples, and many of these in their hearts worship the true God and try to serve Him, but, like Nicodemus, they fear to confess Him openly. Yet frequently such persons boldly confess on their death-beds that they are Christians, and we trust many names not enrolled on our church books will be found in the "Lamb's Book of Life."

We rejoice and thank God for all this, and yet, with you, we are not satisfied, but we long with almost a painful earnestness for more to come to Christ.

தேவன், தம்முடைய ஒரேபேறான குமாரனை
விசுவாசிக்கிறவன் எவனோ அவன் கெட்
டுப்போகாமல் நித்தியசவனை அடையு
ம்படிக்கு, அவனைத் தந்தருளி, இவ்வள
வாய் உலகத்தில் அன்புகூர்ந்தார்.

JOHN III. 16, IN TAMIL.

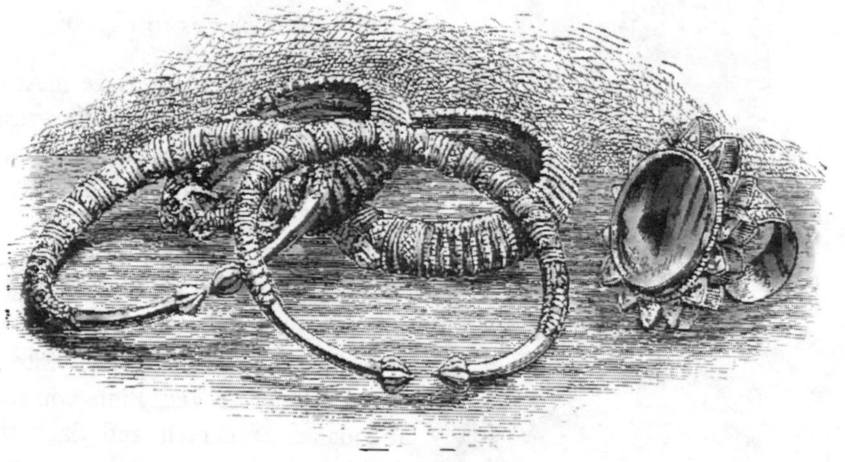

BRACELETS, ANKLETS, AND RING.

CHAPTER VIII.

Mutthuchardie's Money-box.

Manepy, *November 11th*, 1881.

WOULD you like to hear a story of what a Tamil boy did one Sabbath in church, and what came of it?

Some years ago, the native Christians of this mission in Jaffna, Ceylon, formed themselves into a missionary society for the purpose of sending teachers and preachers to the people of seven small islands lying west of Jaffna.

A few Sabbaths ago, in Panditerippu, the native preacher was urging his people to give towards this society. Some of the congregation looked indifferent, thinking perhaps they had enough to do to support their own schools and church; but one little boy, named Mutthuchardie, sitting close by his mother, was listening very attentively, and when he heard that there were many little children on these islands who had no schools, no kind teachers, no books, as he had—that, worst of all, they had no Sabbath-schools, no Bibles, and did not know of the Saviour whom he loved—he looked up quickly in his mother's face and whispered, "Oh, my money-box! You said I might do whatever I pleased with it. Oh, mother! give it, give it!" The mother was astonished that her little boy had understood all the preacher had said. She now began to listen more carefully herself; and

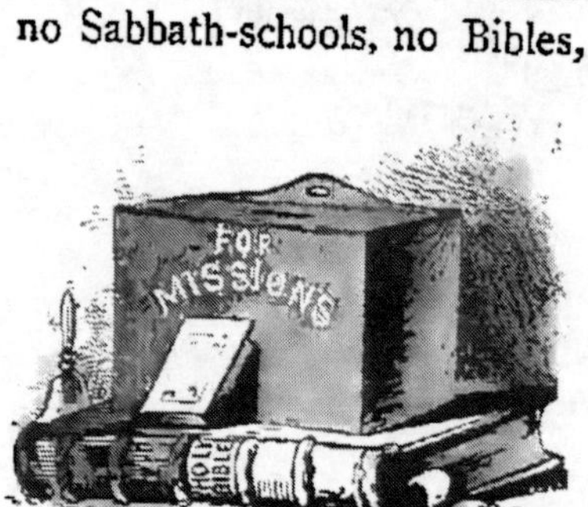

every now and then, as if to emphasize the speaker's words, she felt a soft little pinch on her arm, and heard an eager voice close beside her whisper, "Give it, give it, mother." And, along with the words of the sermon, some other words, spoken long ago, kept coming to her mind: "Whosoever shall not receive the kingdom of God as a little child, he shall not enter therein."

The little boy had his request, for the next Sabbath, when the bag came around, he dropped into it two little fists quite full of cents, half-cents, quarter-cents, and eighth-cents; for we have such small coins here, where so many people are poor and money is scarce. But, when the bag came to his mother, great was the child's surprise to see her quietly slip off her two gold bracelets from her arms and drop them both into the bag. They had come down to her from her mother and grandmother and were part of her marriage-portion, and worth £5. But the words of her only child had rung in her ears all the week, and she said to herself: "I also will give to God and His cause something precious."

Now, as of old, the words of the prophet are true: "And a little child shall lead them."

"And Jesus called a little child unto Him, and set him in the midst of them, And said, Verily I say unto you, except ye be converted and become as little children, ye shall not enter into the kingdom of heaven."

GATHERING DATES.

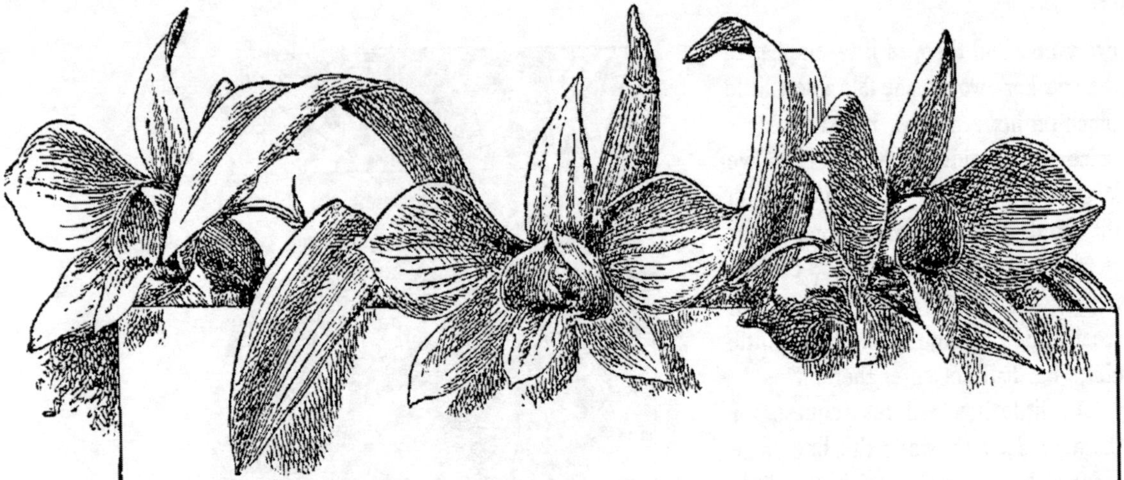

A CHILDREN'S HYMN IN THE TAMIL LANGUAGE.

Subject: Praise to Christ who was born in Bethlehem.

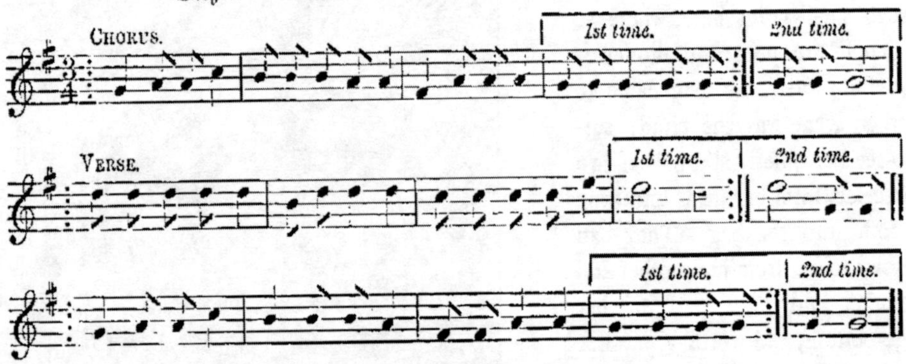

Sound of the Tamil words in English.

CHORUS.

Bĕt-thá-la-yĕl pĕr-ŭn-thă-vá-day
Pót-tē thŭ-thēē mán-ä-may. ĕn-nŭm,

VERSE 1.

Săd-dū-văt-thī-ūm pär-dit-thärn-da
Săd-dū-vă väl-lä-var. ĕng-kay,
Tharl-mī-ūl-la thī-vī-ūt-til,
Thäl-lī sik-kă-lä-nár. ĕng-kay,

VERSE 2

Sing-käs-sän-am veet-te-dŭk-kūm
Thĕr-van min-thăn-ár. ēng-kay
Pang-kam-ut-tä, pas-ŭt thŏd-dē-leel
Pär-dŭt-the-duk-ker-ar. ĕng-kay.

CHAPTER IX.

THE SIVITE PREACHER.

Manepy, *February 7th*, 1882.

I THINK our heavenly Father, when He allows us to feel peculiar trials and discouragements, sends also peculiar encouragements to counterbalance them. Such was your letter to me this morning, for, truly, I was weary in body and mind with the conflicts of a week which has been the hardest I have ever known in Jaffna. I think God knew I should need help, and so put all those loving, helpful words into your heart for me a month ago—another proof of His great, tender, ever-watchful care. I thank Him, over and over, with glad tears, for you and for loving Christian hearts who are praying for us and for Jaffna.

We need your prayers more than ever. Just when in all our schools and villages there was unusual interest, and we seemed almost on the eve of a blessing, what should Satan do but raise up what the heathen call a learned man, a holy man, a great Sivite preacher, who is a most bigoted, bitter, and

A HOLY MAN AMONG THE HINDUS.

unceasing enemy of Christianity? He has sprung up quite suddenly, like a mushroom in the night, and is going about the country breathing out blasphemies and misrepresentations of Christianity, and abuse of missionaries and Christians. Preaching is a new thing to the Sivites. Their priests never preach, their religion consists in forms and ceremonies, and knows nothing of spiritual worship or of edification. His plan of preaching he has copied from the missionaries. Because this is something new, and because he appeals to men's worst passions—pride, hatred, selfishness—he draws great crowds. I suppose he has preached ten or fifteen times in the last few weeks to audiences of from one to three hundred. So long as he attends to all the ceremonial purifications, bathes his body if he touches a low-caste man, eats neither flesh nor salt, and can speak in high-flowing Tamil, which four-fifths of his audience cannot understand—so long as he does all this the people think he is a very great man, and the temple managers throw open their doors to him.

This preacher has spoken twice in the Manepy temple. He began at seven in the evening and continued till nearly twelve o'clock—this is his custom. Do you wish to know what he said? These are his principal points against Christianity: The God of the Christians is not omnipotent, for he took six days to make the world, when it might have been made in one. Jehovah is not omniscient, for He put Adam and Eve in the garden of Eden with Satan, and He ought to have known that they would sin: because He did not prevent their sinning, He is not all-powerful nor all-holy, and therefore Satan is stronger than God. The angels sinned, and fell from heaven: therefore heaven is a place of temptation and sin, and hell is the better place of the two. God is not all-good, because He saves only Christians. It is said that Christ came to bring peace to the earth; but at His birth Herod killed thousands of infants, while He did nothing to prevent it, but ran away to Egypt to hide.

You can imagine what an effect these and similar things would have upon a crowd of the low and ignorant at home. How much greater is the effect on the seething, ignorant, and unreasoning masses here! His last talk was on Saturday night; and on Sabbath morning we found our Sabbath-school boys full of his arguments. We thought that, as wise doctors, we should take the disease in hand at once; so, after hastily going over the lesson, we told them they might ask questions; and for half an hour or longer we answered one after another, until they seemed to see that there was another and better view on all the points. We carried them with us in every step, and never left a point until they understood it. It was the same at Arnikotty, where we teach a Sabbath-school class at half-past ten o'clock, and at Navaly, where we teach one at three o'clock. In this way we met, in the course of the day, between forty and fifty upper-class boys whose minds are in a formative state, and who are

A MAN-EATER.

peculiarly susceptible of impressions. The next few days we visited some of our large English schools; and, being prepared, we took up the Sivite preacher's points one by one, and answered them. We were surprised to see how full they were of his sceptical teaching, and how "men love darkness rather than light, because their deeds are evil."

We told them there were two powers contending for their souls—good and evil; that they might know which was good, because it was always unselfish, and the evil, because it was always selfish. We told them how much had been given and done for them, freely and unselfishly by Christians, and asked if they could show a parallel in Sivism. We told them that the teacher who sent them away with new reverence and love for God, with new longings after a holy life, a determination to fight against sin, was their truest friend, and asked if they left the Sivite meetings with these feelings. We took up the great problem of why God permitted sin, and tried to explain it as best we could, and show how it was better and grander for us to personally, freely, gladly choose the right and refuse the wrong, than to be mere machines compelled to do right without will or choice. We tried to meet the other points, also; but it was a hard task, because the tide against us and Christianity was so strong. Think for yourself what it would be to go into a school of one hundred, all but half-a-dozen of them strong Sivites, from Sivite homes, all bristling with objections, and whether your heart would not be faint and trembling. My sister was the strongest of us all. She has a wonderful way of winning the love and trust of the older boys, and in these days her whole soul has been in what she said; and it was a strange sight to see tears glistening in the eyes of those who were almost men, as she pictured the grandeur of a life devoted to God, urging them to choose that life, and live not for self but for Jesus.

There was one cheering circumstance: the Sivite preacher had said among other things, "The missionaries do not really care for you; they are not your true friends," &c. Over and over again, however, the teachers and the boys, and even bitter heathens, have assured us that he was mistaken; that he did not know us; that everybody in

Manepy knows that we really love the people, and are their friends. I think God has blessed us in winning the confidence and love of this people. To His dear name be all the praise. I realize more than ever the importance of character to support our words, and I am resolved to be doubly careful in all my words and actions, that in everything I may honour Him. My sister says: "Our work for a few days has been in sucking the poison out of the veins of those who have been bitten by the serpent; and we must keep on, day by day, and week by week, until it is thoroughly done."

We are planning to have some of the best speakers in Jaffna go round to the central points in the field and hold large open-air meetings, answering the Sivite's arguments. There is much work for us in the future, for we cannot know just what his movements may bring about, or whether others will join or copy him; but if we will be true soldiers we must contest every inch of ground, and the sight of the enemy will only rouse us to fresh endeavour. We are on the winning side; there is no fear of the result; but the thing that troubles us is the harm that may come meanwhile to some of these boys and girls who are not wise enough to distinguish the false from the true.

THE BANYAN TREE.

Whether it was that by sucking the poison from others we have had a touch of it ourselves, or whether it was being out many days in the midday sun, when the thermometer runs up to 140°—whatever was the cause, last night and this morning I was feeling very tired, and, I confess, a little desponding; but your letter came to do me a world of good.

Later.

I think this movement on the part of the Sivites is resulting in good to the Christians. It is stirring them up to be more prayerful and earnest, and to watch more carefully over their lives. I do not think they are at all affected by the arguments brought forward—they went all over the ground for themselves before they became Christians—but, with us, they are troubled for the results such preaching may have on the young. We arranged two meetings for the 6th and 7th. Two of our best native workers, men of recognized ability and learning, came for both nights. One meeting was held in Manepy, and one at Arnikotty. The total attendance was between two hundred and fifty and three hundred, a majority of whom were high-caste, educated people. The low-caste people—men women. and children—were, in great numbers, busy in the harvest fields, where the rice harvest has just begun, and where they work during the moonlight. So our audience was a thinking one of the higher classes. Two addresses in each meeting were candid, careful answers to questions; the third gave some strong reasons in favour of Christianity; and the fourth was an earnest appeal to seek salvation and a Saviour now.

GIRLS DRAWING WATER.

We were much interested at these meetings in noting the line of argument often followed by the native ministers. One of them, at one of the meetings, laying his hand on the Bible and addressing his audience, said to them, "Many of you do not know what is contained within the lids of this book, but you do know the lives of the missionaries who for so many years have gone out and in among you." He referred to the time when the cholera was prevalent in the peninsula, and asked his hearers to remember what happened at that time. He said, "Many of the people were panic-stricken and left the plague-smitten districts; frequently the relatives of those who were ill fled and forsook them, leaving them to their fate. But what," he asked, "did the missionaries do at that time? Did they forsake those who were in such distress? By no means; they ministered to the sick, they sat by the bedside of the dying, they buried the dead, they counted not their lives dear to them if so be they might render the necessary service. One of the missionaries, the Rev. Dr. Poor, after the most incessant and prolonged service to the sick, at the last fell a victim to the disease and died. His latest breath was spent in praising Christ." The speaker asked, "Is it a good religion or a bad that can produce such a result as that?"

This same Dr. Poor had been for some time stationed in the Manepy district. The speaker asked, "Is there a house in this district which Dr. Poor did not visit over and over again?" He told many touching incidents of this beloved missionary, who laboured in Jaffna for over forty years. Among other things he related how that on one occasion Dr. Poor had been out all day visiting in the villages, and when returning in the evening lost his way. He called to some one who was passing by and asked him if he would show him the way. The man went to get a torch, and when he returned found Dr. Poor on his knees, praying aloud for a blessing on Jaffna. The speaker asked, "Is it a good religion or a bad that can make a man forget his weariness and hunger in the earnestness of his desire for a blessing on the people of another race?"

The speaker referred to the boarding schools, and said, "You feel quite safe in allowing your daughters to be under the care of the missionaries, but would you trust your daughters to the care of a Brahmin? You know you would not, not even for a single night. Is it a good religion or a bad that can make men moral and trustworthy? You always trust the word of a missionary, but you do not trust each other. When you go on a journey, you often prefer to leave your jewellery with the missionary rather than with your own relatives. Is it a good religion or a bad that can make men truthful and honest? Have we not before our eyes the proof that Christianity has the power to do what Hinduism and Buddhism have shown themselves unable to do, to change the heart and to make the man a new creature?" The native minister continued for some time in this strain, and his words, appealing directly to things which all knew, produced a great effect.

On account of the harvest, we shall delay further meetings till the new moon. People who would not otherwise come may perhaps be attracted to hear objections answered, and so be brought under the influence of earnest appeals on behalf of the truth. Will you not pray that the result may be a new awakening in religious matters, and a real turning to God? Oh, that He would make the wrath of man to praise Him by bringing many new souls into the kingdom of His dear Son!

March 18.—I think God has heard our prayer. Our meetings seem to have affected the sober-minded people, and the temple manager has said that he will not invite the Sivite preacher to speak again; that he only deals in abuse, and that the missionaries are the true friends of the people, and ought not to be disturbed in their good work, though they may be wrong in their religion. One boy who has tried to induce others to stay away from Sabbath-school, came yesterday to say he had done wrong, and he was very sorry.

Best of all, the children have been roused to work for Jesus. Last week several came to us privately, asking us to kneel down and pray with them for their classmates, who, they feared, were being drawn away from Christ. We had a number of little seasons of private prayer with them. Last Sabbath, in the afternoon, the children prayed specially for their friends; and at four o'clock three little companies, of their own accord, went into the villages to hold children's meetings. One company had eighteen, and another twenty-four children, as an audience. They came back very much encouraged. I felt that Jesus here, as of old, had taken a child and set him in the midst, and was telling us to be more child-like, earnest, hopeful; and I remembered that other Bible saying, "If these should hold their peace, the very stones would cry out."

Oh, that our lives and words may more clearly ring out the glad cry, "Hosanna! Blessed is he that cometh in the name of the Lord!"

CHAPTER X.

Little Thankam.

Manepy, *April 28th*, 1882.

DID you ever see an idol temple, and a great many people boiling rice for the god? This is just what we see every day in Ceylon.

Just across the road from our home here in Manepy stands a large idol temple dedicated to the god Pulliar. This god has the head of an elephant. He is called the god of wisdom, and when heathen mothers take their children to school, they always bring them first to an image of this elephant-god, that he may give wisdom to the child and make it a good scholar. This is the first god which a great many children are taught to worship. What a pity that they do not know of Jesus, the friend of little children!

In this temple there is a man called a Pandahdam, whose business is to bathe the stone and brass images with milk, cocoanut water, and perfumes daily. He also receives offerings presented to the god. Now this man has one little daughter, and it is of her that I want to tell you. Her name is Thankam Mutthu, or Thankam "for short." The meaning of the name is Gold-pearl, and the child deserves the name, for she is the head scholar among sixty girls in our station girls' day-school. Since she began to come to school she has regularly attended the Sabbath-school, and learned many Christian hymns and Bible verses. Last Christmas, when the Sabbath-school children were examined, she was one of three girls who could say the Golden texts for the whole year, without a mistake. How many children in the home land could do that? She received a prize—a Tamil New Testament—from the Christmas Tree. When she first came to school she used to have some sacred ashes, the marks of the heathen god, rubbed on her forehead, but she left that off after a time, and she studied the Bible so well that she could repeat the whole of the fifth chapter of Matthew without prompting.

Thankam's Sabbath-school teacher—a very lovely native Christian woman—took a great interest in the little girl; and Thankam would steal into her house sometimes and beg her to pray with her and teach her how to serve Jesus. She feared to let her father and mother know of these visits. They wanted that she should learn to read, but they did not want her to become a Christian. They despise the Christians, and consider them polluted because they partake of the Lord's Supper with the low-caste people who have joined the church. They were so very particular that, when Thankam came home from school, both at noon and at night, they would not let her come into the house till she had bathed her whole body at the well. They were afraid she might have touched a low-caste or a Christian child during the day, and so would defile the house.

As Thankam was on her way to school one morning, she called to see her Sabbath-school teacher. While she was there she said:

"I have found a beautiful verse; it says, 'When my father and my mother forsake me, then the Lord will take me up.' That means me, doesn't it?"

Poor child! she did not know how soon her courage would be put to the test. Her father had seen her go into a Christian house. He hurried to the gate and called out, loudly and angrily:

"Thankam, Thankam, come to me."

Thankam looked out and saw him cutting a long switch from the hedge. He seemed to be in a terrible passion, and was uttering the worst kind of threats and abuse.

The poor frightened child clung to her teacher, and the teacher went out and begged that he would not whip the child; but it did no good. He grew more and more angry every moment, and nothing could soothe him. He dragged the child out into the road and there he whipped her very cruelly. The women and children who were standing near could not help weeping as they saw him; they all felt very sad as the little girl went slowly away, and they knew not what would become of her.

For a whole long month Thankam's father and mother kept her shut up in the house, and no Christian was allowed to see her or speak to her. How I wearied to see the dear little face! But it was of no use; to try to see her would only have made her parents angry and made Thankam suffer more; so we and her Sabbath-school teacher who loved her, and the Christian girls in the day-school, told Jesus all about it and asked Him to help her. We knew that He could and would.

After a time the father and mother said they would let her come back to school if she would rub ashes and promise not to be a Christian; but Jesus must have helped her, for she would not promise. She cried so much that at last her father and mother relented and said, "Why should we make our only daughter miserable?" So they allowed her to return without making any conditions.

You would have hardly known her when she came; she looked half starved and so sad; but as soon as she found herself among us you ought to have seen her face shine with joy! From that time blessings seem to have followed the brave little girl, and she has now become a pupil-teacher in the station school.

Will you not pray for the child who begged so hard to come to us, and for the father and mother who are serving Satan so blindly?

PULLIAR, THE GOD OF WISDOM.

CHAPTER XI.

SECOND YEAR'S EXPERIENCE AT THE GREAT HEATHEN FESTIVAL.

Manepy, *May* 10*th*, 1882.

EARLY in the morning our tent had been pitched in our compound very near the temple; an awning had been put up before the veranda of the medical-rooms, comfortable seats provided, and two bookstands had been arranged, giving us in all four preaching-places. At nine o'clock in the morning about twenty Christians gathered together at our house, and after prayer for God's blessing, they took packages of tracts, Bible portions, &c., and went out a mile or more on the different roads to begin their day's work. My brother, with several helpers, took charge of the book-stands and the supply of the sellers; my sister, with a chorus of twenty children and three speakers, took the tent; while the other workers and singers came with me to the medical veranda.

HINDUS BATHING AND WORSHIPPING MUD IDOLS.

At a few minutes after nine we were all ready, and made two openings in our hedge to admit the people, who had begun to arrive in large numbers. Immediately from fifty to a hundred people came into each place; but we had not spoken or sung many minutes before we noticed a commotion in the road. A few bitter Sivites had collected, and, placing themselves in each opening in the hedge, began to sing and shout at the top of their voices, at the same time declaring that no one should go through or enter our yard. At my side of the compound they seated a number of Sivites right across the opening, and at the other side they filled the gap with thorns.

Soon a crowd of hundreds of persons had collected at each place, attracted by the disturbance, and all the more anxious to come in because they were forcibly prevented. Without appearing to notice them, and going right on with our singing, we called our coolies and said, "Open six places immediately in the hedge." It was done, and our opposers seemed rather non-plussed, for they saw that this could go on indefinitely, and that we would cut down the whole hedge rather than give up. There might be a handful of men who would sit all day in the burning sand to stop a gap, but it would need a thousand to encircle a whole compound.

Listeners began to come through the new entrances, and after a little while the whole crowd which had collected broke away in a body and came pouring in upon us. From that time onward we spoke and sang without ceasing to solid audiences of from two to four hundred people. It was very noticeable that they stayed longer and listened better than last year. They enjoyed the speaking and singing, and seemed in no hurry to go. I was also struck with the fact that they were not Manepy people. They were from the islands and distant villages. I saw almost no faces in the audience that I had seen before, and perhaps many present heard something of the gospel for the first time. There was very little disturbance. The general feeling toward us seemed to be a very kind one. I knew they liked what we said; and as we had opened our yard, they gladly availed themselves of it, sitting under the beautiful trees, and thanking us for the shade from the scorching rays of the sun. This insured us good audiences, and our colporteurs had plenty of work visiting and speaking with them.

It is estimated by our workers that one-third of the people did not go to the temple to worship at all, but spent the time with us in the compound. The income of the temple was very small this year—not as large as last year. A reliable man gave me the various items, and the whole came to less than Rs. 140, the total gifts of ten thousand people; while the single Christian church of Batticotta raised at the thank-offering meeting Rs. 180. Our workers are quite jubilant over the day, and say that, if we have two or three more tents and preaching-places next year, we shall absorb a large share of the festival, and many people who appear to be coming to a heathen festival will really be coming to a gospel meeting.

I want to tell you what gave me the most pleasure in this day's experience; it was the way the school-children from six different schools came voluntarily to help us sing.

A TAMIL GIRL

I wish you could have heard their clear young voices ring out the words, and have seen the interest in the faces of those large audiences, many of whom were listening to those sweet Christian songs for the first time. During those long five hours some of the workers became tired, and asked to be relieved; but the singing children, with few exceptions, stayed by to the last, and their bright faces, so eager and willing, were an inspiration to us. At the close they came and said, "Oh, Amma, it has been a happy day." They were having their first taste of working for Christ, and for those whom He loves. Many of them were from heathen families, and two years ago would have worshipped idols themselves. Some of them were children of the *Pandahdams*, who were that very day offering incense to the idol god. These and other children have been severely beaten for not going to temples, and they know that they may be again; but "none of these things move them." The love of Christ has made them brave and strong.

I know that the Good Shepherd will care for them through the rough way, and bring them into His fold at last. Dear friends at home, pray for these boys and girls that they may be faithful, and for the hundreds of other boys and girls who have not yet given their hearts to Christ.

CHAPTER XII.

A BRIEF VISIT TO THE PULNEY HILLS.

Pulney Hills, South India, *June 25th*, 1882.

LET me tell you, first of all, about the annual meeting of the Native Missionary Society, and a concert of Christian songs and hymns in the Tamil language. Both were held on the same day—the 1st of June—at Batticotta Church, the largest one in North Ceylon. All the morning the church and the mission compounds were gay with the arrival of crowds of happy people in hackeries, horse-bandies, ox-bandies, and on foot. The men were dressed in flowing white and the women in gay-coloured robes, and there were a great many little children. These, with the boarding-school girls all in white like vestal virgins, and the young men from the Jaffna College with the unmistakable wide-awake air peculiar to college-boys, made a very pretty picture.

It was an all-day meeting, and both the forenoon and afternoon sessions were full of interest. The audience was a fine one—over six hundred men, four hundred women, and several hundred children. As I sat on the platform, to play the organ, I had a good view of their faces, and a more intelligent gathering of people I never saw. Of the one thousand and twelve communicants in this mission there are only about thirty who cannot read. Most of the audience had been through the higher schools, and were well educated. This Native Missionary Society, which carries on work in the neighbouring islands, has been officered and managed by natives for the past thirty years. It is probably the oldest missionary society in Ceylon or India which has been supported and conducted by native Christians for so long a period. For the past year the funds raised, mostly from native sources, amounted to Rs. 872.13. On this day the collection came to Rs. 150. The reports of work done in the islands during the year by one pastor, one catechist, and several day-school teachers, were encouraging. A fine large map, twelve by sixteen feet, of the seven islands, the field of the society, drawn by the secretary and hung before the audience, was an appeal through the eye to the heart. The addresses by the four native speakers were very good; and those by Rev. S. W. Howland, of Oodooville, and Rev. J. C. Chandler, of the Madura Mission, were specially interesting. At the afternoon session the Lord's Supper was administered.

As the concert was to be on the same evening, about two-thirds of the people stayed to attend, and the native Christians of the Batticotta Church most kindly and generously provided for all an abundant meal of rice and curry. It was their own plan, carried out with true hospitality, and with the putting aside of caste prejudices, which was a real triumph of grace. In the meantime, bandies from all directions, and crowds of people, began to arrive for the concert. The church was brilliantly lighted; the organs and choirs of singers were arranged in the centre, and the rest of the large church was filled with every available seat that could be obtained within a circle of three miles. The people poured in until every seat and every inch of standing-room was taken, and then they overflowed into the road. More than two thousand people were present. The singers, in all, numbered over one hundred, being choirs from the two girls' boarding-schools, the training-school, and the Jaffna College, with some little children from Manepy and Oodooville day-schools, who sang some songs specially adapted for infant voices. For instruments we had two organs, played by the Rev. Mr. Chandler and myself, three violins, one flute, bagpipes (native make), drum, and cymbals. When all the instruments and all the voices came in on the four chorus pieces it was very stirring. There were no failures, and everything passed off better than I expected. The little children from Manepy sang out as sweetly and clearly as little bells, and were repeatedly cheered by the audience. The thirteenth lyric, sung by three tiny boys between six and seven years old, with two older boarding-school girls from Oodooville, and a violin accompaniment played by a boy about eleven, was very prettily rendered. This hymn represented a conversation between a mother and child about the slaying of the infants by Herod and the escape of Christ into Egypt. The tenth lyric, which was very long, more like an oratorio, and contained twenty-four different movements or tunes in four different keys, was sung by the students of Jaffna College. The audience was very quiet and attentive throughout, and we felt that they spent an enjoyable and profitable evening. To the multitude of heathen present a pleasant and attractive phase of Christianity was presented, and the sweet story of Jesus told in song could not fail to open a door in some hearts.

The same evening we, with Mr. Chandler and his singers, went on board the boat for India. At our last helpers' meeting in Manepy, when they knew we were going to be absent from them for a little time, instead of being discouraged, they gathered around us, and said: "We will do our very best when you are gone. We will keep up the moonlight meetings and the school-work just as it is going on now, and you will find everything all right when you come back." We have had some very good letters from them since we reached the Pulney Hills. We landed at Negapatan, in India, about noon on the following day, and left in the six o'clock train. Train! Was it not grand to feel one's self flying away, propelled by steam once more! It was a beautiful moonlight night, such as only those in the tropics know, and I sat hour after hour watching, as we flew on and on past trees, and fields, and towns, intoxicated by the swift motion, and the wild, free, glad feeling which it brought, as if some heavy burden had been dropped—an anchor lifted, a cage-door opened, and I, a white-winged ship or a bird flying before the wind. In the morning we found ourselves passing through an interesting country. I could hardly realize that I was in the great country of India—this strange, this storied land.

Coming up through the hot plains of India, what a joy it was to catch sight of the glorious mountains, towering up between seven and eight thousand feet, and to think

A BATHING-PLACE.

of the cool, clear, invigorating atmosphere inswathing their tops! It is a comfort to know that there are such cool places in this hot land. How delightful it was to see mountain scenery again, after two years and a half on an absolutely flat plain—for I was cradled in the lap of the grand old New England hills, and in sight of my home, stretching away to the east, were the peaks of the White Mountains, snow-capped for nine months in the year—the Delectable hills of my childhood.

GOING UP THE MOUNTAIN.

These Indian mountains ascend almost perpendicularly. We were carried up, as the custom is, in chairs borne upon the shoulders of four coolies. They go, in a zig-zag path, right up the side of the mountain, the whole length of which, from base to top, is twelve miles. We started from the foot at about four o'clock in the morning.

How delightful it was to hear again the sound of roaring mountain brooks dashing over the stones; and how good the pure, cold water tasted! What a luxury! I had forgotten that water could be so cool, or taste so refreshing.

How can I describe to you the delights of that cool, misty morning? The fresh mountain air fanned our brows. The birds overhead, as if in rivalry to the singing brooks, broke out in melody: every little throat seemed bursting with song. The mountain-tops loomed up majestic and mysterious in the mist.

Now we came into the heart of the jungle, and great forest trees, many of them entirely strange to me, stretched out their large arms over us, their stateliness relieved by the many kinds of creepers that in tropical luxuriance ran and clambered everywhere, making the thickets dense and shady; and underneath I spied the most beautiful kinds of ferns. They say there are eighty different varieties of ferns

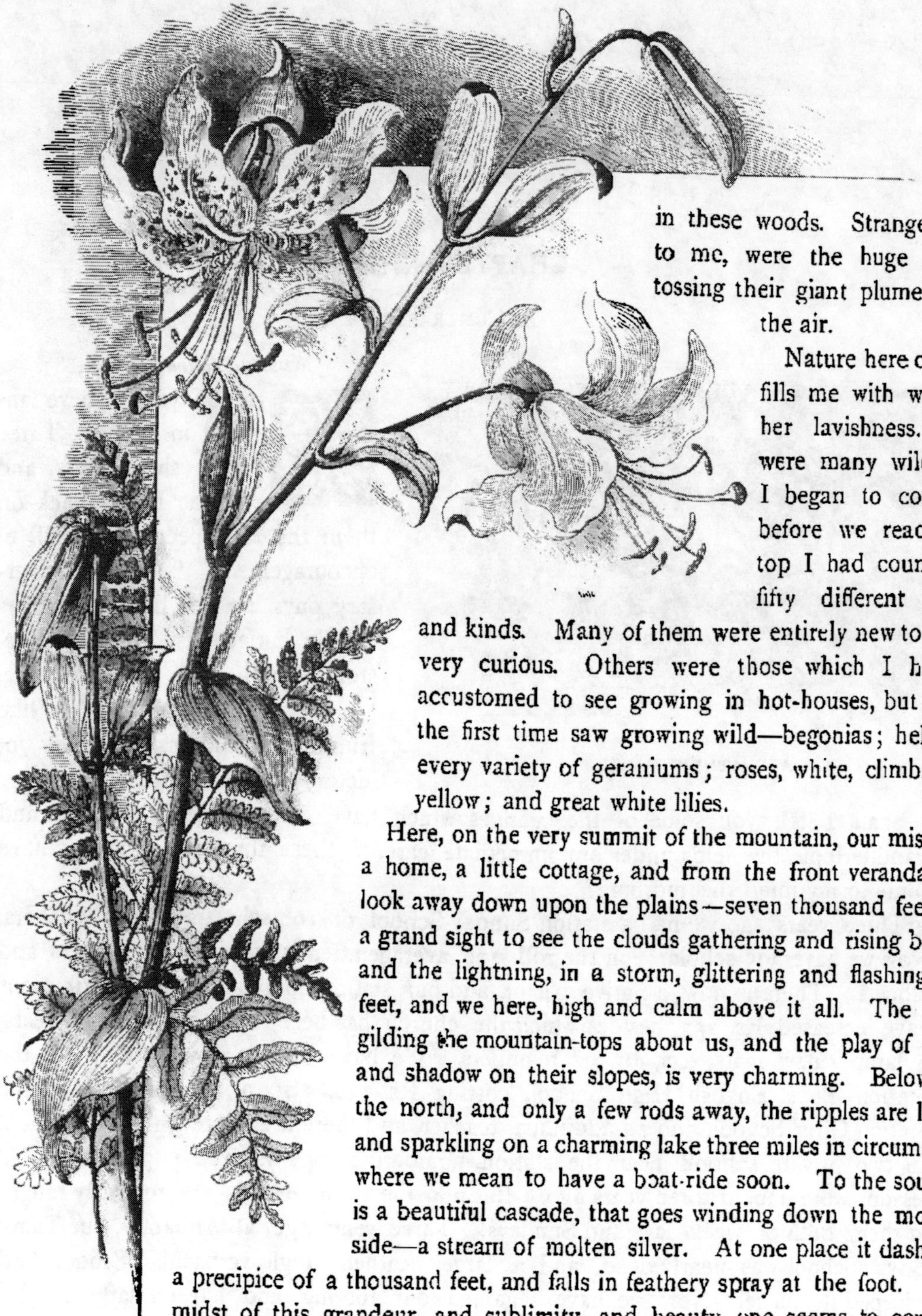

in these woods. Strangest of all, to me, were the huge tree-ferns tossing their giant plumes high in the air.

Nature here constantly fills me with wonder at her lavishness. There were many wild-flowers. I began to count, and before we reached the top I had counted over fifty different varieties and kinds. Many of them were entirely new to me, and very curious. Others were those which I had been accustomed to see growing in hot-houses, but now for the first time saw growing wild—begonias; heliotrope; every variety of geraniums; roses, white, climbing, and yellow; and great white lilies.

Here, on the very summit of the mountain, our mission has a home, a little cottage, and from the front veranda we can look away down upon the plains—seven thousand feet. It is a grand sight to see the clouds gathering and rising below us, and the lightning, in a storm, glittering and flashing at our feet, and we here, high and calm above it all. The sunlight gilding the mountain-tops about us, and the play of sunlight and shadow on their slopes, is very charming. Below us, to the north, and only a few rods away, the ripples are laughing and sparkling on a charming lake three miles in circumference, where we mean to have a boat-ride soon. To the south-west is a beautiful cascade, that goes winding down the mountain-side—a stream of molten silver. At one place it dashes over a precipice of a thousand feet, and falls in feathery spray at the foot. In the midst of this grandeur, and sublimity, and beauty, one seems to come very near to God, and to be filled with adoration at the thought of His power, and wisdom, and love.

CHAPTER XIII.

A CONTRAST.

A HEATHEN FAMILY.

Manepy, *January 14th*, 1883.

THREE years ago we landed in Jaffna. Three very short years, and yet as I look back on them the retrospect seems full of encouragement. "These anniversary days are not like tombstones of the buried past, but like milestones, marked on the other side, 'so much nearer the goal,' or like triumphal columns, trophies of victory 'won for Jesus.'"

Shall I tell you some of the changes which have taken place in Manepy and Panditerippu, the fields under our immediate care, in these three years, as they have come to my mind this morning?

Three years ago we had a station Sunday School of 100 scholars and 5 teachers. Now we have 395 scholars on the roll, 200 average attendance, and 21 teachers and officers. There is now a native pastor, and our station church annual contributions have increased Rs. 257, besides which the church has been furnished with 10 seats, 9 lamps, new mats, &c., by its members. We have a fine new building for the Station Boys' English High School, costing Rs. 350, also a new building for the Station Girls' School, and an additional teacher, and there are more children in each. In two private schools near the station, numbering together 160 pupils, no Bible lessons were taught three years ago. But now the Bible lessons are regularly taught in them, both on week-days and Sundays. Three years ago, at Arnikotty, our Tamil Boys' School was nearly dead, and a large heathen Anglo-vernacular School had usurped its place. Now we have regained our footing, and have a large Anglo-vernacular School, with 5 teachers and 125 boys who are taught Bible lessons, and are brought to the Sunday School.

A new girls' school of 60 children has been organized at Suthumalay, for which a new school building was erected and furnished. We also have a new building for the Arnikotty Girls' School. We have an additional teacher at the Arnikotty South Mixed School, and 28 more scholars. The Bible is taught in the Arnikotty West School of 68 children, where it was not three years ago. In Navaly Station Girls' School we have an additional teacher and 36 new scholars. The Navaly Church building has been finished and repaired, and new seats and mats added, at a cost of Rs. 162. We have there a Sunday School of about 175 average attendance, against 75 three years ago.

In North Navaly we have a new Girls' School, with new building and furniture, and 60 pupils. We have a similar Girls' School with new building and furniture, at Santillipay. A compound has also been bought there, and a bungalow erected at a cost of Rs. 265. A new catechist is stationed there, who conducts regular Sabbath and week-day services, and superintends a Sabbath School with an average attendance of 50.

At Panditerippu Station, the average attendance at Sunday School is increased by 25. The church building has been repaired and the floor relaid at a cost of Rs. 721, also new seats and a new pulpit introduced at a cost of Rs. 75. In the Panditerippu Station English Boys' School we have an additional teacher, and a much more flourishing school than three years ago. In the Sirruverlan School we have a new building, an additional teacher, and 31 new scholars.

To sum up in a few words, we have under our care 3 more day-schools, total 27; 14 more teachers, including sewing teachers, total 57; 395 more pupils, total 1865. The above does not include two private schools before mentioned, which also co-operate with us. The Bible lesson is taught in seven schools where it was not taught three years ago. At the close of last year, a most carefully conducted review Bible-examination showed 1565 scholars examined, and the total of Bible verses recited from memory 8831, and of questions of various catechisms 42,736. We have now in our Sabbath Schools 94 teachers, and 1529 pupils on the list, a gain of 881 over three years ago. In the annual review examination on the International Sunday-school Lessons, held in last December, 244 pupils recited the golden texts for the whole year, 27 for three quarters, 49 for two quarters, and 125 for one quarter. Our church membership has increased 40, total 190. The contributions of the three churches in our field were Rs. 454 more this year than three years ago.

We have sent from our field to the Jaffna College, Training School, Girls' Boarding Schools, and other higher institutions of learning, 49 young men, 38 young women. Many of these decided to give themselves to Christ while in our day and Sabbath

A CHRISTIAN FAMILY: THE KENWAR AND KENWARANI, OF KAPARTHALA, AND THEIR BOYS.

schools, and 54 of them have already joined the churches connected with these higher schools, or have applied for church membership. 757 Bible portions in Tamil, and about 50 New Testaments in English, were bought from us by the day and Sunday-school children. Many more were bought from the depository, besides several hundreds given out as Christmas rewards. 468 religious tracts were sold, and 5565 tracts and 1514 handbills distributed during the past year. Three years ago we had only 4 Bible-women, now we have 9. They report having visited 409 houses regularly during the past year, besides teaching Bible lessons, sewing, and singing to the girls in nine day-schools, and holding many cottage meetings. They are teaching 125 women and grown girls in their homes to read the Bible. These have memorized altogether, during the year, 2070 Bible verses, 209 hymns, and 1458 questions, which must have given them employment and food for thought in many otherwise vacant or unhappy hours. Of these women and girls, 39 have begun to pray to Christ, and, we hope, to love Him. If you read between the lines in these statistics, if you try to make the facts real in your mind, I think you will be encouraged, as we are, and hopeful and prayerful about the future.

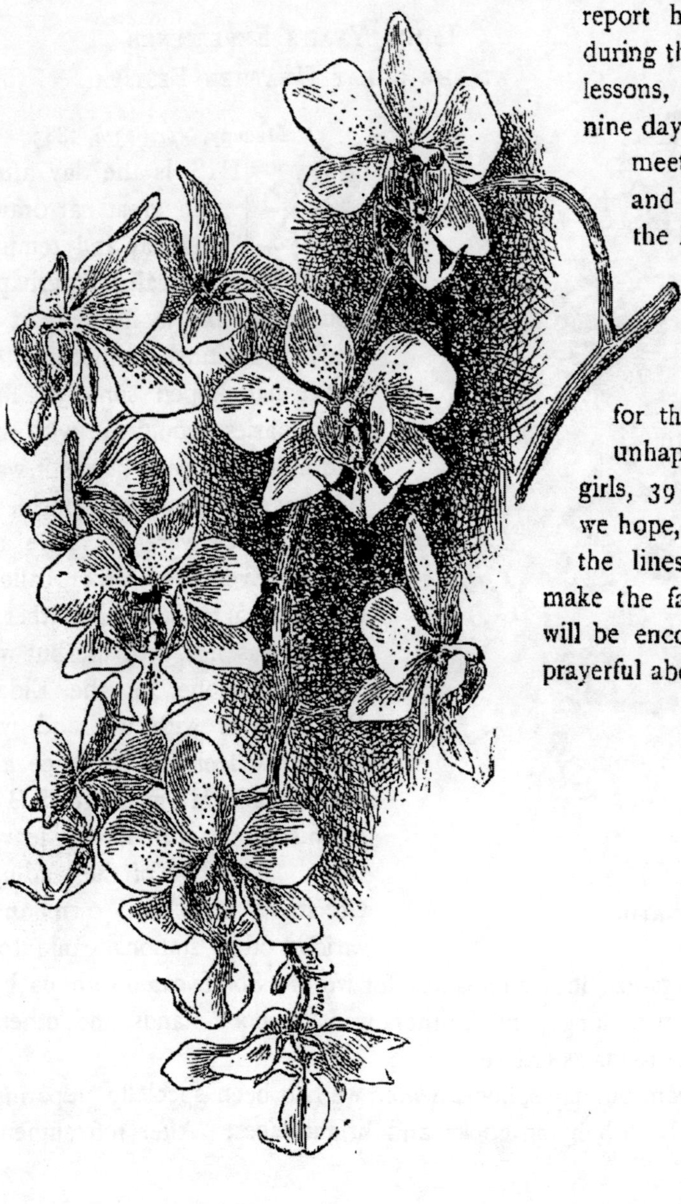

CHAPTER XIV.

THIRD YEAR'S EXPERIENCE AT THE GREAT HEATHEN FESTIVAL.

THE CAR OF JUGGERNATH.

Manepy, *April 13th*, 1883.

THIS is the day after the great car-drawing day and temple festival; and perhaps you would like to hear about it and our meetings on that day.

We had hoped some of the missionaries would be with us and assist this year, but as it was the day of the quarterly business meeting they were not able to come. Even our brother, called to America by our dear father's illness, was not with us, but we were not alone, for the Elder Brother was with us, and we seemed to feel His presence all the day, and He made good His promise, "I will never leave thee." About 30 of the leading Christians from our own and various other stations came together in the morning to organize into companies for work. Some came with us by invitation to the tent and preaching pandal, others went to book-stands, and others went out a mile or so on the roads as last year.

Also about 40 children from our day schools, whom we had been specially preparing for this occasion, came early with hymn-books and bright faces. After refreshment

BRAHMAN FAKIR ENGAGED IN MEDITATION.

and prayer we all began work at 10 a.m. My sister went to the tent, and I to the medical veranda, where a large pandal had been erected and seats provided. Our children's voices, joining in a bright ringing hymn accompanied by organ, violin and cymbals, soon brought us large audiences.

We had eight of the best speakers we could get in Jaffna, four with each of us, and they did indeed speak well, so simply and earnestly, relieved every little while by the children echoing their words in some appropriate song.

This year—although there had been some talk beforehand that there would be opposition, that Sapapathipullai the Sivite preacher would be present to speak, that heathen tracts would be distributed, that they would not let any one enter our yard, that they would dispute at our meetings—although there had been some such floating talk and some articles published in Sivite newspapers to that effect, yet God must have been specially with us, for none of all these things happened, and we had altogether quieter and better meetings than last year. No one tried to hinder people from coming, or to disturb our meetings, but people came in large numbers and stayed longer and listened better and went away more quietly than last year. Many stayed from an hour to an hour and a half, and even longer. Many thousands of people found a refuge from the burning sun in our veranda, tent, and under the large shade trees, and some spoke gratefully to us for allowing them the privilege. Thus we won much good feeling and many seemed to enjoy our meetings, and I hope some carried away real good.

On the white wall of the veranda we had painted in Tamil in large scarlet letters these verses: "*God is love.*" "*Blessed are the pure in heart, for they shall see God.*" "*There is joy in heaven over one sinner that repenteth.*" "*Come unto Me, and I will give you rest.*" Those who came from a distance toward the meeting seemed struck with these verses shining out from the white wall, illuminated by the noon-day sun. They would begin to read, and I could see their lips move and their eyes follow the lines as they read one and another, and they would come nearer and look inquiringly at the speakers as if to say, "Can you explain these?" And the speakers explained them, weaving all they had to say about them, and pointing to them and reading them over and over again. Thus they served a second purpose of which we had not thought when having them written—they unified all the addresses. These four verses were silent preachers of repentance, purity, peace, and love to thousands during the day; surely they must be remembered in some hearts. Our little singers did beautifully; they sang off and on for five hours, their little throats growing tired at last, but their faces still shining.

Mr. Twynam, the English Government Agent of this province, came on from town in the afternoon to see if all was quiet, and if the headmen were at hand and preserving order; for there are disturbances among the people at such large festivals; and I think our opening our grounds and calling in so many of the people, thereby lessening the crowd about the temple, has tended to preserve quiet and to prevent fights.

He drove slowly past the temple just at the time when they were drawing the car, and instead of the people opposing his passing, to our astonishment hundreds upon hundreds forsook the idol car to walk after his carriage, a mark of their high respect for him, and their really small reverence for or faith in the idol.

Mr. Twynam sent his salams to us, said he was glad we were having meetings, and told us to go on, and all the headmen heard him say so. He asked to hear my little folks sing, so I sent fifteen or so of my station school children in the care of a pastor to him. The great crowd which was about him was attracted by the sound of the violin, cymbals, and the children's voices, and thus my little folks held for a quarter of an hour the largest service of Christian song during the day, with the highly respected Government Agent as the centre. We thank God for the success of the day, and pray that He may bless all that passed to the good of some of the many who were present.

WORSHIPPING KALI.

A STREET IN CEYLON LINED WITH TAMARIND, COCOANUT, AND OTHER TREES.

CHAPTER XV.

A Letter from a Christmas Tree.

Manepy, *December 25th*, 1883.

DEAR CHILDREN,—I am a Christmas tree which you helped to plant in Santillipay.

I am not a spruce-tree such as you use in your country, as I am told, but a tamarind-tree with very beautiful soft foliage like a fern, and a very valuable and plentiful acid fruit. A tamarind-tree is one of the largest kind of trees in this country, and one of the most valuable; a full-grown tree sometimes produces £1 worth of fruit in a year. But a *tamarind Christmas tree* produces still more valuable fruit, for the toys with which I am covered delight a hundred little eyes, and the Tamil Bibles and Scripture portions and hymn-books will feed the heart.

I grew in the mission compound in Santillipay, and after the roof of the large preaching bungalow was all lined by the teachers and native Christians with white cloth, and after a beautiful arch of strung red and white oleander blossoms was erected and other decorations put up, I was brought in and planted. Immediately the children brought more flowers, limes, plantain fruits, &c., to decorate me. Then the gifts sent by you, and prepared by the missionary ladies with the name of the future owner written on each, were hung upon me, as well as lots of little bags full of popcorn, roast peas, roast rice, native sugar and sweet cakes. These were brought and hung till my branches were bending down with the heavy load. But the merry shouts of the children helped me to keep up a stout heart and not give way.

Then the missionary ladies arrived, and to their surprise they were met by a large company of people, and a native band of music consisting of five instruments, two flutes, large and small, a kind of native bagpipe, a drum, and cymbals.

A canopy of red cloth decorated with flowers was carried over the heads of the missionary ladies, rose water from silver vases was sprinkled over them, and flowers, two large baskets full, were strewn before them. This was all arranged as a pleasant surprise by the people, to show their goodwill and love. Was it not a great change from the year before last, when at some moonlight meetings the missionary ladies and Christians were stoned, the fruit-trees belonging to a Christian family robbed, and their fowls killed? At that time all the boys in the place were studying in a Sivite school in which the secular lessons were taught on the Sabbath as well as on week-days, and where the students were taught to mock at Christianity. Now there is a Mission-school here with 120 children, where the Bible lessons and Christian hymns are daily taught, and the children are brought on the Sabbath to Sabbath school and church service.

These children were all present around me, and they were seated on ola mats spread on the floor. They were all dressed in their best clothes, and, as bright colours are much liked by the people, they looked like a flower garden. Their little baby brothers and sisters came also, and many of the fathers and mothers as well. These were all seated around the four sides of the building. The boys and girls were prepared with many dialogues, recitations, compositions, &c., appropriate to the occasion, in English and Tamil, all of which they recited very well, I thought. Some were about Christ, His birth, His teachings, &c., and one boy in the midst of his address opened the Bible and read a part of the Sermon on the Mount, and all the heathen present listened with attention to those beautiful and lofty words. There was much singing, Miss Leitch had her "American baby organ" with her, and also a part of the Manepy children's choir with violin and cymbals.

Then several persons present gave addresses. After this the presents were distributed. Quite a number of boys and girls whose names were found on the "roll of honour," because they had recited perfectly the 145 Bible verses, twelve hymns and lyrics, and fifty-two golden texts, which formed the Bible lesson for the year, as well as shown a perfect or nearly perfect Sunday School attendance, received prizes of

New Testaments or hymn books. Have any of you little girls and boys to whom I write done as well as they, and do you stand on the roll of honour?

After the meeting all the men, women, and children escorted the missionary ladies half a mile on foot toward their home, walking in procession and headed by music.

My work is done. A coolie has come to cut me up for firewood for the catechist's family, so in death as in life, I am,

Your faithful
CHRISTMAS TREE.

A VIEW IN CEYLON.

A BANYAN TREE.

CHAPTER XVI.

The Week of Prayer

Manepy, *January 14th*, 1884.

LIKE the banyan tree, the Kingdom of Christ seems to be growing and extending here, taking deeper root downward, and sending new shoots upward.

We were much encouraged this year during the week of prayer. The English-speaking children from our large English schools at Manepy and Arnikotty came into the meetings, not reluctantly as last year, but always with a glad rush. On the last day, after several addresses, in which they were urged to decide for Christ now, they were asked how many wished to give their hearts to God at the beginning of the new year, and many hands were held up.

The Christians took new courage, and in their evening meeting said, "Let us save the children, and in ten or fifteen years, instead of one or two hundred Christians in this field, there will be thousands." The Christians consecrated themselves anew to

Christ's service with earnest prayers and tears, and we are looking for a blessing on the work this coming year. We distributed during the past year twenty-four copies of D. L. Moody's book of sermons, and a large number of his tracts, and we see they are having an excellent effect. We expect to have the book translated into Tamil, and printed before next Christmas. You ask, "Do you see signs of His coming footsteps?" I answer, "Yes, yes; there are everywhere signs of His coming. I can see the fields white for the harvest." The question I would send back to my friends is, "Where are the reapers?" During the past week, which was the week of prayer, my sister and I attended thirty meetings. But there were calls from villages for Gospel meetings which we could not attend. How are my sister and myself to direct the teaching of the Bible lessons to nearly 2000 children in schools? In our field are nearly 20,000 people, and every village open for the Gospel, and calling for moonlight meetings. We have had the Christians, not only men but women and children, organized into companies to go to these meetings, but they are not enough. At any of these meetings, if sister or I can go, from one to five hundred will attend. Formerly a missionary had to go through a village and call the people, and he thought he was successful if he could get a dozen or two to listen to him; but now, when the fields are ripe for the harvest, we are short of labourers.

A BIBLE-WOMAN.

I am just now enjoying very much accompanying our dear native Bible-women, and visiting the homes usually visited by them, and going over the Bible lessons taught by them during the last three months. I think they are doing very good work. I see real progress in the women whom they visit—not only that they can say more Bible verses, but that they show more earnestness and more desire to know God, and more wish to serve Him. I have hope that in many hearts there is true love for Christ. Though fear of husbands and friends and custom keeps them from coming out to Church, or openly acknowledging Him by joining the Church, *yet they do acknowledge Him in their homes and before their families and friends, and are known in their homes as women who do not go to heathen temples or rub ashes, but who study the Bible and pray.* Let us rejoice in this, and pray the Lord to give them strength for the other part, which is, oh, so hard in this country! You at home cannot know the strength of customs and caste prejudices here, or how difficult it is to break away from these. I wish you could go with me to these homes and see these bright faces, and hear the words of welcome, and see the serious earnestness with which they at once sit down and recite their Bible lessons. I cannot help thanking God, again and again, that we are granted the great privilege of sowing the precious seed of His Word in so many willing hearts. I hope our friends at home will continue in prayer for this work.

At the annual meeting of the Jaffna Auxiliary Bible Society, recently held in the town of Jaffna, I heard an English Church missionary relate an incident which had been told him by a missionary from China, and which has been in my thoughts a great deal since. He said that in the China Inland Mission the work in some places seemed very hard and discouraging, but in one native church, under the care of a native pastor, there were always inquirers and conversions and additions to the Church, and this was so remarkable as to excite the attention of many of the workers in China. One of the missionaries of that mission on going home to England was met by a gentleman from Bristol, who invited him to his house, and surprised him by asking him the most careful questions, showing a remarkable and thorough acquaintance with the work. In the course of the conversation it became known that this Bristol gentleman had undertaken some time ago the support of the native pastor before mentioned, and had sent the funds regularly through the society on condition that this pastor should send him very frequent accounts of the work in all its details. The missionary said he understood the secret of the success of that work when he heard this gentleman pray. He prayed for the young converts by name, he prayed for the inquirers, stating their various difficulties, he prayed for the pastor and for the native Christians. He prayed as one speaking to a dear and tried friend, and sure of an answer. And he was answered. God had in a wonderful way honoured that man's intelligent and believing prayer. When I heard it I could not keep back the tears. We want such believing prayers offered for Jaffna. It seems as if we could not do without them.

"The Lord's hand is not shortened that it cannot save, neither His ear heavy that it cannot hear." Is it indifference and unbelief which have kept back the blessing which He was willing and waiting to give?

"*God be merciful unto us, and bless us, and cause His face to shine upon us.*" "THAT THY WAY MAY BE KNOWN UPON EARTH, THY SAVING HEALTH AMONG ALL NATIONS. *Let the people praise Thee, O God: let all the people praise Thee. O let the nations be glad and sing for joy.*"

CHAPTER XVII.

PROTECTION IN TIME OF DANGER.

Manepy, *July 4th*, 1884.

JUST five years ago to-day we left our Vermont home and turned our faces toward Boston and the foreign field.

We are celebrating the day in what is to us a very joyful manner, viz. in seeing twelve persons examined by the committee for Church membership They will join on profession of faith on the coming Sabbath. There are a number of others who have asked to be received, but it was thought best for them to wait till next occasion, in order that the Christians may have time to know them better and have fuller proof of their sincerity. I trust they may prove true.

Last April and May the smallpox broke out in several of the villages around us, making it necessary for us to close a number of our day-schools for a time, but not one of our Christians or Sabbath School children, as far as we know, has suffered. At the time nearly 2000 children were learning the 91st Psalm : "He that dwelleth in the secret place of the Most High shall abide under the shadow of the Almighty," &c. This lesson had been fixed months before for this time. Was it a coincidence only that the precious words should come to give courage in time of danger? Was it not a special providence that none of our dear people were stricken? Yes, the special Providence whose love plans every moment of our lives, and therefore in life or death nothing can go wrong with us.

A few months ago a Christian girl lay dying of fever. She said, "I do not want to stay ; I want to go, for heaven is better." A little later she said, "Mother, I see in heaven they are giving in their accounts," and a moment later, "I see my little sister there;" and stretching out her hands she died with a glad smile. Her father a native Christian lawyer, has just given Rs 750 in memory of his two daughters, to found two scholarships in the Wesleyan Girls' Boarding-School where they studied.

This is an index of how true a hold Christianity has on the hearts of native

Christians here. Many in years to come, in the name and for the sake of these dear departed ones, will receive the blessings of a Christian education in this Girls' Boarding-School.

***

After reaching Ceylon one of the first things which affected me very deeply was the sight of a heathen funeral. On going to the house where a little child had died, I found the mother beating her face on the ground and wailing most piteously. *The human heart is just the same all the world over, and mothers love their children. This poor mother had no hope of ever seeing this child again or taking it in her arms or knowing it as her child, and her heart was breaking.* Soon the little body which she pressed so convulsively to her bosom would be carried away by the men of the village and reduced to ashes in the burning ground, and the ashes would be strewn in the sea. She thought the child she loved was lost to her for ever, and the future seemed all dark to her. Very often mothers, under such circumstances, will refuse to eat food for days together, and sometimes a mother's hopelessness and despair are such that she commits suicide.

Dear mothers in the home land, some of you have lost a little child. What did you do in that sad hour? You went into your closet and looked up into the face of your Christ, and poured out all your sorrows before Him. You remembered that He had said, "Suffer little children to come unto Me, and forbid them not: for of such is the kingdom of Heaven." You thought how He had taken up little children in His arms and blessed them, and you believed that your little one was safe and happy with Him, that He was caring for it better than you could care for it, that you would see it again, and your hearts were comforted. Was it not so? *Remember there are other mothers who need the same comfort which comforted you in your hours of great sorrow.* Oh, make haste to tell the heathen mothers of Jesus, the Almighty Saviour, the infinitely compassionate One, for they need Him as much as you do.

Some time after we landed in Ceylon I attended a Christian funeral. Again it was a little child that had died. I looked into the faces of the father and mother, and although their eyes were full of tears, I saw a look of *hope* on their faces. A number of native Christians had come to the house, and we joined together in singing Christian hymns. The native minister came and held a brief service. Then all followed the body to the grave-yard, walking in procession and singing in the Tamil language:—

> "There's a land that is fairer than day, and by faith we can see it afar,
> For our Father waits over the way, to provide us a dwelling-place there.
> In the sweet by-and-by we shall meet on that beautiful shore.
> In the sweet by-and-by, we shall meet on that beautiful shore."

We stood around the open grave, and the native minister opened the Bible and read those words of Christ's: "I am the Resurrection and the Life: he that believeth in Me, though he were dead, yet shall he live." Marvellous words! Surely none but a Divine Saviour could have spoken words so suited to meet the needs of the human heart. I looked again at the faces of the father and mother; they were upturned to heaven, and I saw in them a look of *resignation and peace.* In my heart I thanked God that we had such a Gospel to give to the heathen—a Gospel which presents such glorious hopes. Our dead are not lost, but gone before. We shall meet them again on the other side, and there shall be no partings there, "and God shall wipe away all tears from all eyes."

CHAPTER XVIII.

A Christian Wedding.

Manepy, *July 11th*, 1884.

TRAVELLING CART.

WE had a very large Christian wedding in our church the other day It was attended by at least 800 people, many of them from amongst the highest families in Jaffna. The father of the bride years ago came from a high heathen family, to study in the mission boarding-school. To enter there, one of the subjects for examination was the Scripture catechism. Although his father was a stiff heathen and had his son taught in a private heathen school, yet he sent him to a Christian village school for a few months, just in order that he might learn the Christian catechism and pass a good examination.

This was the beginning of his knowledge of Christianity. He then went to study at the Batticotta Seminary (a school which preceded the Jaffna College), and while a student there he became convinced of the truth and was brought to Christ When his parents knew this they were very angry, and threatened him with the loss of his inheritance On the Sabbath, when he was to have been baptized, they shut him up and took away all his clothes. When, later on, he received baptism, he was cast off by his parents, but our mission sent him to Manepy, where he studied medicine under the late Dr. Green. He is now the leading native Christian doctor in Manepy. and has a large practice and wide reputation.

He married a Christian girl, having refused offers from the parents of much richer heathen girls. He has now a large, fine stone house, and an interesting family of children. His wife is a very lovely woman, beautiful in person, in mind, and in heart. It is a joy and satisfaction to have her company and help in village meetings. or in visiting in the homes of the pupils of the Bible-women. She teaches a class of girls in

A NATIVE GIRL.

A LITTLE BRIDESMAID.

Sunday School, though most women with a family of six children, three of them little ones, would not think they could come promptly at 8.30 a.m. on Sabbath mornings as she does. She goes out every Sabbath afternoon to hold a women's meeting in the neighbouring village, taking her little children with her.

The eldest daughter, about whose marriage I began to tell you, is a beautiful girl, nineteen years old, educated in the boarding-school, speaking English, able to read music and play on the organ, and a good singer; she sews and embroiders, and is a good housekeeper; but more important than all, she is an earnest, loving Christian.

A young man related to a high heathen family, who studied in the Jaffna College and became a Christian, asked for the daughter in marriage, because she was a true Christian. When this young man's parents heard of it, they were very angry. They wished him to marry a rich heathen girl, and return to heathenism. They offered if he would do this to give him £300, and the relatives offered £100 if he would marry with heathen ceremonies. He refused, and chose to cast in his lot with the Christians. The persecution of his friends was so great that he felt he must either accede to their wishes and become a heathen, or else leave his home, which he did. His mother threatened to throw herself into the well, and his father threatened to disinherit him, and finally they sent him word that they regarded him as one dead.

It was very trying that not one of his immediate relatives was present at his marriage, but the Christians and the missionaries and many educated and influential natives were present, to the number of 800. The marriage was celebrated in the Manepy church. I was glad that so many should have the opportunity of seeing a Christian marriage, and hearing the words of the native pastor and our missionaries. It was nearly dusk when they left the church, Christian lyrics in Tamil composed for the occasion, and sung with accompaniment of native instruments, having very pleasantly filled up the time.

As the bridal party left the church, garments were spread before them the whole way to their home, an arch of flowers was borne over their heads, a band of music preceded them, and the whole company of people accompanied them on foot in the brilliant glare of torches, blue and red lights, rockets and fireworks, provided by friends to grace the occasion.

We hope that they may have a very happy and useful life, and carry out their intention of devoting themselves directly to Christian work in connection with this mission.

THE OODOOVILLE GIRLS BOARDING-SCHOOL.

CHAPTER XIX.

PERSECUTION AND DELIVERANCE.

Oodooville, *January*, 1885.

NEAR the close of last year we were stationed at Oodooville, a place about a mile distant from Manepy, and in addition to our other work we were given the charge of the Oodooville Girls' Boarding-School. Will you not pray that grace may be given us to meet these added responsibilities ?

The past year has been one of much encouragement. Fifty-nine persons have united with the three Churches in our field, namely forty-five in Manepy, eleven in Navaly, and three in Panditerippu. Besides these, quite a number from our field, former members of our day and Sabbath schools and inquirers' classes, have been received on profession of faith in the Wesleyan and Church Mission churches, and are now students in the boarding-schools of those Missions. In all this we rejoice. Our native Christians, at the beginning of the year, during the week of prayer, united together to pray that fifty might be brought to Christ within the year. Some thought it was a very large request, but it was the prayer of faith from more than one heart. They now feel that God has heard this prayer, and they take courage to ask for great things this coming year. We do not forget that dear friends in the home-land have been praying especially for this field and work, and we are glad that these prayers have been and are being answered, and we believe that we shall rejoice together at the last great ingathering.

Another encouraging feature of the year has been the forming of several new inquirers' classes. There are now held weekly seventeen such classes, with a total average attendance of about 150. In these meetings the portion of Scripture appointed to be read during the week is explained. Each one is expected to repeat a verse of Scripture and to offer prayer. The leader also inquires after and encourages each one in the class in regard to habits of daily prayer, Bible study, and church attendance. The classes are conducted by the native pastors, catechists, leading native Christians, and by ourselves. To join one of these classes helps the young people to take a step toward confessing Christ, puts them under the care of older Christians, and thus, by meeting together from week to week, they become a band of friends to encourage each other. They also become known in their villages as inquirers. Inquirers' classes are rallying points to which any one showing signs of interest is at once invited. In countries where to leave idolatry and come over to a public profession of Christianity is so vast a change, such a class as a stepping-stone is a great help. It is our desire to see an inquirers' class, however small, in every day-school before the end of the coming year. For God's help in this, and for these 150 inquirers, we ask our home friends to pray.

The religious history of some of those who joined the church this year seems to us interesting. I will mention a few instances.

Chelappah, a man in Arnikotty, was led to Christ by the persistent efforts of a young Christian boy. He has shown so much earnestness in regard to bringing up his family, as quite to put to shame many of our older Christians. He brought his wife and children to church. He did not make the common excuse of want of jewels and beautiful clothes, and though the heathen relatives persecuted and ridiculed him, he took no notice. He had his children baptized. He bought a whole Bible and began family prayers. He sought the Bible-women and invited them to teach his wife. He brought his daughter often to the girls' inquirers' class, walking the mile both ways and waiting patiently outside during the meeting. He had the joy of seeing his wife join the church at the close of the year.

One of the inquirers, a young man of a high heathen family, has lately achieved a great success in being married without heathen ceremonies. The parents of both parties were strong Sivites, but the young man never for a moment wavered. The bride had formerly learned the Bible lessons in our day-school, and again, when too old to go to day-school, i.e. after the age of twelve, she had been taught in her home by one of our Bible-women, so she also favoured a Christian marriage—one of the many good results of Bible-women's work.

Another, a young man of the Pariah caste, who had studied in one of our day-schools, was threatened by the higher-caste heathen people, his former masters, with dreadful punishments if he should join the church; for the old system of master and serf, though under the English Government it is done away with in name, still exists in a greater or less degree, and the Pariahs stand much in fear of, and are in subjection to, the higher castes. For three years he hid the light in his heart, living privately as a Christian, but fearing to confess Christ. At last the light would not stay hid, and he joined the church. The next Sabbath he was stopped on his way to the morning service and ordered to work, and beaten because he refused. He still continued to attend church, and because of this, one day when on his way to town with a bundle of cloth to sell, he was caught, robbed of his cloth and earrings and waist-chain, compelled to walk ten miles in the hot sun, and left in a strange village, with threats that if he ever returned to his home he would be imprisoned. This was done, it appears, to intimidate other low-caste people from becoming Christians, lest they should become enlightened and no longer submit to heathen control. The youth stayed away some weeks, and then ventured back and still continued to attend church. His late masters then instituted a false case against him in court, but through the efforts of our native Christians it was abandoned, though both parties were fined a considerable sum for non-appearance. The heathen people were enraged that they had to pay this sum, and forthwith dragged the youth to their house and made him stand for three hours in the mid-day sun, with his face turned toward the sky and holding a stone on his forehead—a most cruel torture. On learning this, we warned the people that if they committed another act of violence toward him they would be prosecuted. On the next Sabbath the youth, notwithstanding threats and punishments, was found in his place in church both morning and evening. The lesson in Sabbath School was about Paul's willingness not only to be bound but also to die for the name of the Lord Jesus, and I noticed, while teaching it, that his face was shining as if with the very light of heaven. Poor youth, I little thought how soon another trial would come to him! On the very next day those men took him to their house, and, tying his hands and feet, beat him in the most shameful manner and left him bound in that way for some hours. My sister was called by a relative and saw him in this state. The moment she had left him in order to seek for help, they, fearing she would take a case against them, dragged the youth for some distance over the dust and stones on his bleeding back, which was unprotected by any clothing, and then marched him off to town over fields and fences a round-about way, for fear that others would see them, their object being to get a false case into court before we could enter a true one. But their plan did not succeed, for my sister saw the police inspector the next morning, and the magistrate at once gave orders to have the men arrested and sent to jail, with the prospect before them, if the case were tried, of being sent to prison for a term of years. They begged for mercy, which for the sake of peace in the village we thought best to grant, but they had to pay fines and costs, &c., amounting to about Rs. 100, I think, and they have promised in future to let the youth alone. The incident has proved a complete success, for if any low castes wish in future to join the church, they will feel at liberty to do so. The people of that village have learned several lessons. And I want to say that all along the self-control, firmness, and courage of the youth were admirable, and showed what Christianity could do even for a Pariah.

TAPAL RUNNERS.

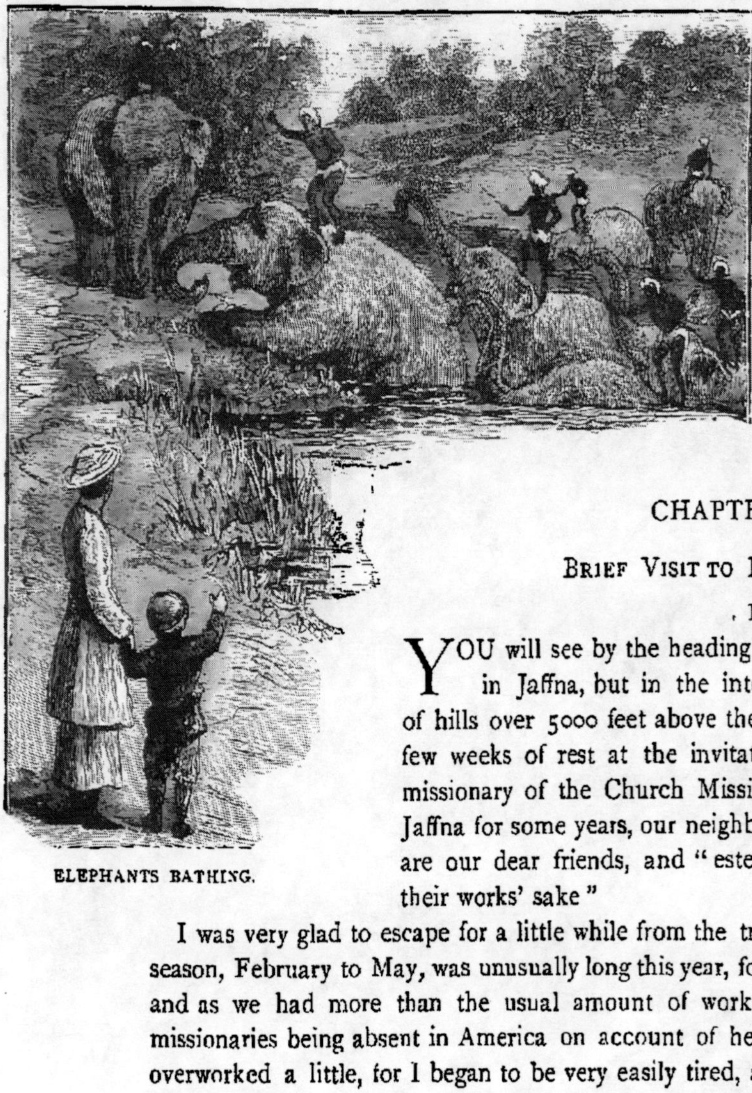

ELEPHANTS BATHING.

CHAPTER XX.

BRIEF VISIT TO NEWERA ELLIA.

Newera Ellia, *July* 30th, 1885.

YOU will see by the heading that I am not at this moment in Jaffna, but in the interior of the island, on the top of hills over 5000 feet above the sea. I have come here for a few weeks of rest at the invitation of a lady, the wife of a missionary of the Church Missionary Society. They were in Jaffna for some years, our neighbouring fellow-workers. They are our dear friends, and "esteemed very highly in love for their works' sake"

I was very glad to escape for a little while from the trying heat of Jaffna. The hot season, February to May, was unusually long this year, for the wind was late in coming; and as we had more than the usual amount of work on our hands, three of the missionaries being absent in America on account of health, I suppose I must have overworked a little, for I began to be very easily tired, and to feel unable to go on with my duties. Now, after a little perfect quiet and freedom from care, in this delightful climate, with the beautiful wooded hills all about me, reminders of the dear home land, and a pleasant change from Jaffna which is quite flat, I feel my old self again, am able to eat and sleep well and to take long walks of two or three miles morning and evening. I shall soon return to Jaffna, and when this letter reaches you, you may think of me as back again at Oodooville with our 108 girls in the boarding-school, and with sister, who has been finding it a little hard to be without me. But she has been going on with the work nobly, having large moonlight meetings and women's meetings, also a thank-offering meeting, besides the Sabbath-school, whose

A VIEW IN CEYLON.

A TREE FERN.

numbers have now swelled to 340. I long to be back again. I shall return with new courage, and hope to make up for my short holiday by the renewed vigour with which I shall be able to go on with my duties. Sister has had three Christian singers over from India during my absence. Two were from the Madura Mission and one from Trichinopoly, South India. The latter chants the psalms beautifully, using the Gregorian or Free Chants, which are very easy, and which are liked much by our native Christians, and thus God's words are becoming more known and precious. The Madura men have been teaching some of the beautiful new Christian hymns and lyrics lately composed in South India, adapted to native tunes, collected and arranged by the Rev. J. S. Chandler, of the Madura Mission, and published in Madras by the Religious Tract Society. The singers brought over 3000 copies, which are being eagerly bought up by our native Christians, day-school children, and even the heathen community. These new songs are being widely learned and sung—one of the easiest and best ways of diffusing Christian truth. When I return to Jaffna we hope to arrange for a large public concert of Christian song, such as has been held on two previous occasions.

Now I will tell you a little about my present surroundings, which I think are very beautiful. The house in which I am is situated on the shore of a little lake, some four miles in circumference. This lake is nestled in the lap of the hills, which surround it on all sides. There are three beautiful little waterfalls in sight, winding down the sides of these hills like silver threads, and reminding me of the waterfalls I saw in Switzerland when we were on our way to Ceylon. There are many well-kept carriage drives and walks all about, for this place is the Government Sanatorium of the island, and there are about forty European residences, besides the native village. The Governor and his suite come here in the season. Then the place is very gay.

My hostess—when the pony is at home and not in use by her husband on his preaching tours in the surrounding estates—takes me out for long and pleasant drives of from six to twelve miles in the afternoons, which I much enjoy, and we come home with our hands full of wild flowers and ferns. The air is mild, and the thermometer is at 65° in the middle of the day indoors. So we sit with doors and windows open, and the perfume of flowers floating in and filling the air with fragrance. Flowers grow here so easily, and many varieties are in bloom in the garden surrounding the house. Some of them are old home friends. The most lovely budded roses of all varieties thrive well. Mignonette, fuchsia, and geraniums grow here into tall shrubs higher than my head. Peach-trees have both blossoms and fruit at the same time. Orange-trees hang golden with oranges. Several kinds of Australian trees, having been introduced into the country some time ago, now grow and flourish everywhere. Great tree ferns, tossing their huge soft feathery plumes twenty to thirty feet high in the air, grow all about, and are my constant wonder and admiration. There are many kinds of ferns here; I am making a collection in my walks, and pressing them to send home.

The tropical sun retains its old power even here, and one cannot long be out under it unprotected without getting a headache. Some people, deceived by the cool air, go out in the middle of the day and get sunstroke. One man, a little while ago, was struck down to the ground, had to crawl home on his hands and knees, and was ill for a long time afterwards. all because he walked out in the sunshine without a pith hat or umbrella.

All this interior part of Ceylon has by English industry and capital been converted into huge tea and coffee and cinchona estates. Thousands of Tamil coolies come over from India, and are employed on these plantations. There is a railroad from Colombo to this place, and a small steamer goes round the island twice a month. It is by this steamer that I will return from Colombo to Jaffna.

THE COFFEE PLANT IN FLOWER AND FRUIT.

A NATIVE BOAT.

CHAPTER XXI.

ITINERATING ON THE ISLANDS.

Oodooville, *March* 31, 1886.

WITHIN the fourteen months since we wrote to you, sixty have joined the Oodooville church on profession of faith, thirty from the villages, and thirty from the boarding-school. It was an interesting thing to see young girls with bright, earnest faces, young lads in the promise of manhood, fathers and mothers with their little children in their arms or clinging to their garments, old men and women feeble and bowed with age, one leaning on his staff, all standing up together, the rich and the poor, the high and the low, together confessing before all the congregation their faith in Jesus the Saviour of the world, their one Lord.

At present the list of inquirers connected with this church alone numbers 130. A copy of the list is given to each of the leading church members, with the request that they will pray for and encourage these individuals. Two meetings for inquirers, one for women, the other for men, are regularly held every Sabbath immediately after the morning service.

In Oodooville, Manepy, Navaly, and Panditeripu, we had altogether ten Christmas-trees, and gave away to the Roll of Honour children 102 Tamil New Testaments. Will you not pray with us that God will bless His own Word to these young hearts and in so many homes? The well-filled home-boxes received from America just before Christmas lightened our labours greatly, and made the occasions very happy ones to hundreds of pleased recipients. Could the children at home who prepared the gifts have seen the joy of all the little ones here who received them, I think they would have felt repaid for their trouble. The more expensive picture-books, beautiful scrap-books, work bags, &c., which seemed too choice for the village children, proved just the thing for prizes for the girls of the boarding-school, who were glad to carry them home and show them with pride to their friends. The total attendance at all our Christmas-trees was over three thousand—men, women, and children.

On February 15 the Oodooville Girls' Boarding-school closed its school year, graduating a class of twenty-four girls, all professing Christians. The public exercises were attended by several missionaries and by a large number of native friends, including many of the leading educated men and women of Jaffna. One could not help noting how large a number of the women present were graduates of this institution. Their faces showed the pleasure they had in revisiting their Alma Mater, and listening to the recitations and songs of their children now in the school. All the graduating class took part in the exercises, eighteen giving short English recitations, and six reading Tamil essays on the following subjects: The Women of India, The Wonders of the Nineteenth Century, The Power of Christianity, Lord Shaftesbury, The Duty of the Women of Jaffna in Regard to Temperance, and The Class History and Valedictory. The exercises were varied by frequent songs—a Tamil lyric, a motion song, a children's English play-song, a tonic sol-fa round, a chant, two English part songs, and a good-bye lyric composed for the occasion and sung responsively by the graduating class and the school. Six girls also in turn played on the organ, accompanying the singing. At the close, the chairman, the Rev. Dr. Hastings, made some appropriate remarks, in which he pictured the condition of things in Jaffna in 1816, when the missionaries first came. Then not a single woman or girl in the whole peninsula could read. Now there are nearly 5000 girls studying in mission schools, 400 of whom are studying in Mission Girls' Boarding-schools, and there are over 1000 Native Christian female communicants in the different mission churches, many of them actively engaged in work for Christ. We may well exclaim, "What hath God wrought!" He then presented to each of the class a diploma, a Tamil Reference Bible, and a lyric and hymn-book. Nineteen prizes were awarded for general scholarship, as well as for

SHORE LINED WITH PALMS.

needlework and deportment; eight for punctuality and attendance; three for instrumental music; four for neatness of person and dress; and two for cooking. The occasion seems to have been enjoyed by all. In the Government Grant Examination held a few days ago, the school passed eighty-four per cent., and earned 2450 rupees.*

The day after the graduating exercises of our boarding-school, I took a trip to islands lying south-west of Jaffna. These have a population of 28,000 people. I took with me our tent, folding organ, violin, cymbals, and five singing children, a native pastor, a catechist, a Bible-woman, and two young men, one a student in

* This school receives no aid from any missionary society, excepting the superintendence of the missionaries. The expenses of the school are met by the Government grant, the fees of the pupils, and the interest of an endowment and scholarship fund. We have secured subscriptions toward this fund, mostly from native sources, of Rs. 15,000. Of this Rs. 7100 have been already paid, and the remainder is to be paid in monthly or quarterly instalments through a period of years. Friends of this school in America have most kindly sent to us or paid to our brother sums amounting to £160, which has been invested for the school.

the Theological class and one a teacher in the Tillipally Training School, also our magic-lantern and Bible pictures. We visited and held meetings at three of these islands, but spent most of our time on the island of Delft. This, on account of the meeting of different currents within a mile or so of the shore, is quite difficult of access, and although sometimes visited by missionary gentlemen, it has never before, within the knowledge of any one living there, so I was told, been visited by any white lady. The people seemed delighted to see us, and we had on the evening of our arrival a meeting of perhaps one hundred and fifty—men, women, and children. We showed our magic-lantern pictures; first, the birth of Christ, explaining about the coming of Christ and our need of a Saviour; then the beautiful pictures of Christ blessing little children, raising the dead, and giving sight to the blind, the Sermon on the Mount, the returning prodigal, &c. All listened with attention and great interest. After this we held meetings each morning and evening, and visited the people in their homes during the day, but not in the middle of the day, as the sun was too hot to permit our going out; but at that time the people, at our request, visited us. This island contains about 2000 people. The most of the lower castes have become Roman Catholics, but all the others are Sivites. There is a good school here, supported by the Native Missionary Society, with an attendance of about fifty children taught by a Christian teacher. There are as yet no converts on the island, except a young boy, Canapathy Pullay, belonging to one of the highest families. He was converted while studying under this teacher. He is now studying in our English school at Manepy, and we hope when he shall have finished his studies he will go back as a catechist to work on his native island. This young boy was at home while we were there, and was very diligent in helping to arrange for our meetings and in calling his friends to attend them. His grandfather is the most influential man on the island, and is now engaged in building an expensive heathen temple. I passed it in company with Canapathy Pullay as we were calling people to a meeting, and as we looked at it he brushed the tears from his eyes and said: "I wish my grandfather would become a Christian." It is said that, if this man should become a Christian, most likely many of the people of the island would give up heathenism. It has been a great joy to us to know the firmness with which this young boy, Canapathy Pullay, has adhered to Christianity, refusing in any way to participate in heathen rites or ceremonies. The grandfather said to me: "Take the boy; he belongs to you; he has given up his old religion." The boy's mother and her four sisters, all respectable married women and much adorned with jewellery, came to see me. They told me the boy had said I was his mother, and that I was kind to him, and so they wanted to see me. I told them that if I was the boy's mother, then it must follow that they were my sisters.

They seized the idea with apparent delight, and, putting their arms around me, covered my hands with kisses in the native manner, that is, smelling them as if smelling a rose or something fragrant. I told them that if they were my sisters, they must become Christians. They have consented to let Canapathy Pullay's sister and cousin join our boarding-school next year. His sister is a beautiful girl, and has as sweet a smile as any perhaps I have ever seen on a child's face. We also took with us on our return to Jaffna a cousin of this Canapathy Pullay, to join the Tillipally Training-school.

I think our meetings were greatly blessed. Of those who attended, eleven expressed a wish to be baptized, and to be known thenceforth as Christians. We formed them into an inquirers' class, and asked them to go regularly every Sabbath morning to the teacher's house to be instructed. One of the inquirers, when asked why he believed in Christ, answered with emotion: "I have heard of our gods fighting great battles and doing many wonders, but I have never heard of their loving us and dying to save us." These high families seem to be all related, and I believe that when they begin to become Christians they will all come together. The people were very kind and hospitable to us. When we visited a house the first question usually asked was: "What can we give you?" and forthwith they would have a cow or a goat, or perhaps a buffalo, lassoed and brought to the door and milked, and would give us fresh milk to drink. They drew the milk into a hollow bamboo-stick and we drank it from a folded plantain-leaf.

We enjoyed our stay very much, and the people seemed sorry that we should leave. Some of the women clung to me and said: "You must stay with us." This I would dearly have liked to do but for my much-loved work in Jaffna. But I thought of my wealthy sisters in more favoured lands, some of whom could be spared from their homes. They are spending their time perhaps over music, painting, or such things, all well enough in a way, but I wished they could know something of the supreme joy of having a child or woman with a dark skin, but bright, intellectual face, look up into theirs with a grateful gaze and say: "You have made known to me my Heavenly Father." Could you bring from the piano a strain of music as sweet as that? Could you draw on a canvas a face that would shine like such a face? A painter once said to me: "My great grief is that my pictures cannot breathe or speak, that the heart cannot beat or feel." But you might draw pictures on faces that speak, and on hearts that feel. We bade the people farewell, promising to visit them soon again if possible.

CHAPTER XXII.

GNANAMUTTHU.

Oodooville, *April*, 1886.

OF the 120 girls who are now studying in the boarding-school, fifty are Church members and seventy are not. Many of those who have entered the school this year were from heathen families, and some had never really heard of Christ before. A little girl from one of the islands, when we told her of heaven, asked in great wonder if we had come from there.

To lead these girls to Christ, and to form in them a Christian character which will stand the test of the sore trials to which they will surely be exposed hereafter—"Who is sufficient for these things?" and the time so short. Every year girls drop out from the different classes, never to return to the school. Often our girls are taken out of the school to be married. Their heathen parents will try to marry them to heathen relatives. What we do must be done quickly and well. Will you not specially ask for us and ours God's blessing? We thank Him daily for giving us so large a number of dear ones to train for Him. It is a happy work. It is His work.

April 30th.—Jesus has called one of our dear girls home to Himself. She was a day-scholar of the boarding-school, and lived with her parents, who are Christians, only two or three compounds from us. She was sick but a few days and her death was quite unexpected, but the Master came and called for her. It is a joy to us all to feel sure that she was ready to go. Though only nine years old, she had learned to love her Saviour and to work for Him also. Her older brother joined the Church at the last communion, and this dear child Gnanamutthu begged hard to join, but her parents thought she was too young. Now they are very sorry. Gnanamutthu (Wisdom Pearl) was a member of the Young People's Society of Christian Endeavour and one of the "Look-out Committee," and a faithful little worker. The subject for our next meeting,

MISS M. W. LEITCH AND TAMIL GIRLS.

appointed at our last, is "Heaven." How little we thought that before the next meeting came to be held one of our number would be called to enter there! How dear and real has the place now become!

Gnanamutthu used often to call her school-mates and hold little prayer-meetings in her own or neighbouring homes. The priest of a neighbouring Sivite temple told us that when his little son was very sick, Gnanamutthu came to the house, and kneeling down by the sick child prayed so earnestly for his recovery that all who heard it said it seemed as if she were talking with God, and as if He were very near. The child recovered, and the father believes it was in answer to her prayer. This morning, on going to the funeral-house, I found there thirty or forty of the heathen neighbours who had come in of their own accord, according to the custom of the country, to mourn for the dead. These women were beating their breasts and tearing their hair, and swaying their bodies back and forth, and all together uttering piercing shrieks. This they will do for seven days, gathering together morning and evening. Their cries can be heard a long distance off. At my coming they became quiet, and I spoke to them of Jesus, the friend of little children. I told them of this child's faith in Him, of the joy and peace He had given her in sickness, and of the glorious happy home to which we believed He had taken her. They gathered close around me and listened with eager, hungry looks. Many of them had lost little ones, and they asked if I thought they would ever see them again. One said her little babe had died, but she supposed it would come again to this world in the form of a snake or a rat, or some other animal. The Hindus believe in 8,400,000 transmigrations. How glad I was to tell those hungry mother-hearts of a better hope, a hope that their dear infants were gathered in the Saviour's arms, to "go no more out," but to be for ever safe and sheltered in His bosom, and that this Saviour was their Saviour too if they would but come to Him, and that He had taken their little ones in love that they might follow after.

When I left the house one of the women walked home with me. She said that, since the death of her two Christian children, she had lost faith in idols and had left off going to temples, and now she wanted to worship the Saviour they worshipped, and to meet them in heaven.

> "Let sorrow do its work,
> Send grief and pain;
> Sweet are Thy messengers,
> Sweet their refrain,
> When they can sing with me
> More love, O Christ, to Thee,
> More love to Thee."

A CHILDREN'S OUTDOOR MEETING.

CHAPTER XXIII.

THE YOUNG PEOPLE'S SOCIETY OF CHRISTIAN ENDEAVOUR.

IT is a striking truth which is embodied in the familiar saying, "The boy of to-day is the man of to-morrow." If we as Missionaries and Christian workers wish to win and hold this country for Christ, we must win and hold the children, for the boys and girls of the present will be the men and women of the future, the not distant but *near* future.

A little boy, when asked derisively by some one, "What are little boys like you good for?" replied, "Please, sir, little boys like me are the stuff they make men of." His answer was one which every worker for Christ and humanity would do well to lay to heart. Work for the children is the strategic point in our campaign. Men and women in heathen lands are bound by the trammels of custom and habit, their minds are darkened by superstition and worldly wisdom, and their consciences hardened by sin. But the child's heart is open and tender, and if saved and won to Christ it is not a half-wasted life but a whole life saved and won.

Two questions had long been pressing on our minds in connection with the work for the children, viz. how could we best foster the spiritual life of the native Christian children and train them into useful and active Christian workers; and how could we lead heathen children to take a first step toward Christ, by giving up heathen practices and voluntarily placing themselves under Christian influences? On reading a book entitled "The Children and the Church," by the Rev. F. E. Clark, of Boston, founder of "The Young People's Society of Christian Endeavour," we were led to feel that the methods of this society, which had proved so successful in America, were adapted to heathen lands as well, and as a result three societies bearing this name and having the constitution and bye-laws of the parent society, and with a membership of 170, have been formed in different parts of our field. The object of these societies is, "To promote an earnest Christian life among the members, to increase their mutual acquaintance, and to make them more useful in the service of God." The members consist of two classes, Active and Associate, and the President, Vice-President, Secretary, and Treasurer, are chosen from among the active members. All candidates applying for active membership are required to sign the following pledge (I append the revised version) :—

> Trusting in the Lord Jesus Christ for strength, I promise Him that I will strive to do whatever He would like to have me do ; that I will make it the rule of my life to pray and to read the Bible every day ; that I will support my own church in every way, especially by attending all her regular Sunday and mid-week services, unless prevented by some reason which I can conscientiously give to my Saviour, and that, just so far as I know how, throughout my whole life, I will endeavour to lead a Christian life.
>
> As an active member, I promise to be true to all my duties, to be present at and to take some part, aside from singing, in every Christian Endeavour prayer-meeting, unless hindered by some reason which I can conscientiously give to my Lord and Master. If obliged to be absent from the monthly consecration meeting of the society, I will, if possible, send at least a verse of Scripture to be read in response to my name at the roll-call.

In the three societies formed various committees have been appointed from among the membership, viz. the Prayer-meeting Committee, Sabbath School Committee, Missionary Committee, and, most important of all, the Look-out Committee.

It is delightful to see how heartily the young people enter into the spirit and work of the society. Oftentimes the native pastor, catechists, and teachers attend the weekly prayer meetings, and when they see in the one brief hour of the meeting every member as far as possible *present* and taking *some part* either by offering prayer, reciting a verse of Scripture, or speaking a few words relative to the appointed subject, a look of renewed hope comes into their faces, such as might be seen on the faces of old veterans when they behold the approach of reinforcements.

On Sabbath mornings all the Endeavourers are present in their various Sabbath schools, which are growing through their efforts. After the Sabbath school comes the morning service, when the native pastors give to their people good, plain, gospel food, and the Endeavourers sit with their Bibles in their hands ready to turn up the passages read or quoted. But in order that the native Christians may not get "spiritual dyspepsia" by eating too much gospel food and doing too little gospel work, Sabbath afternoons are devoted to direct efforts in behalf of the heathen around. At about 3.30 p.m. small companies of Christian men may be seen going out in different directions, north, south, east, and west, to hold evangelistic meetings or to conduct Sabbath schools in the surrounding heathen villages, and with each company of men may be seen three or four Endeavour boys, who go to help in calling in the people and with the singing. In the same way companies of native Christian women, three or four in a company, may be observed going out in different directions every Sabbath afternoon to hold meetings in different villages among the heathen women, and with every company of women go three or four Endeavour girls to carry the Bibles and hymn-books, to help gather together the heathen women and girls, to aid in the singing, and to act as little nurses to any crying babies, so that the mothers may be able to listen without distraction. Many meetings are thus held every Sabbath afternoon by the native Christians, attended by hundreds of heathen.

We earnestly desire to see a large working force developed in our Churches. In the great fight of light against darkness, truth against error, we must gather together and enlist the young, fresh energies of the Church. "Trained under the arch of a solemn covenant daily to read the Scriptures, and pray in secret to God, and weekly either to offer public prayer or bear public testimony in honour of Jesus Christ as their only Redeemer," we trust they will go out to fight the good fight of faith as brave soldiers of the Cross. If India and Ceylon are to be won for Christ, and won soon, every native Christian, high and low, rich and poor, old and young, must be enlisted as a warrior. It has been said that seven-eighths of all who have been brought to Christ in China have been won by the efforts of converted Chinese, and perhaps the same proportion would hold true of converts in Ceylon and India. A Hindu gentleman, after listening to an able address from a native pastor, made the following comment :—"Once a forest was told that a load of axe-heads had come to cut it down. 'It does not matter in the least,' said the forest. 'They will never succeed.' When, however, it heard that some of its own branches had become handles to the axe-heads, it said, 'Now we have no longer any chance.' So," said this gentleman, "as long as we only had foreigners to deal with we were safe, but now that everywhere our own countrymen are enlisted on that side, certainly our faiths are doomed." This utterance is significant as showing the impression made upon the Hindus when the Gospel is preached to them by converted Natives.

If the hope of the speedy evangelization of India and Ceylon lies in the native agency, then surely the training from earliest childhood of those on whom are soon to devolve such great responsibilities is a task worthy of the best efforts of the most devoted missionaries.

We all remember the story of the famous master at Eisenach, John Tribonius, who used to give his lessons to his pupils with uncovered head, and when asked why he did this, he replied that it was to honour the consuls, chancellors, doctors, and masters who would one day proceed from his school. " Though you do not see them with their badges," he used to say, " it is right to show them respect." And in that teacher's school at that time was a boy whose words, when a man, were to shake the world; the boy Martin Luther. I think, as I look into the faces of the young people of the Endeavour Society, " These boys will some of them be pastors, catechists, or teachers one day, and these girls will be wives and mothers in the homes, teachers in the Sabbath schools, Bible-women, and Christian workers." Now, when their religious instincts are so strong, their consciences so tender, their young hearts so willing and eager, with what care, with what prayer, with what love, should they be nurtured and trained for the service of Christ and the Church.

In this great work for the conversion and Christian nurture of the children, may we not confidently look for the blessing and help of Him who took up little children in His arms and blessed them, and who said, " Suffer little children to come unto Me, and forbid them not, for of such is the kingdom of heaven "?

THE MAISTER AND THE BAIRNS.

BY A YOUNG SCOTTISH POET.

The Maister sat in a wee cot hoose
  Tae the Jordan's waters near,
An' the fisher fowk crush'd and croodit roun'
  The Maister's words tae hear.

An' even the bairns frae the near-han' streets
  War mixin' in wi' the thrang,
Laddies an' lassies wi' wee bare feet,
  Jinkin' the crood amang.

An' ane o' the Twal' at the Maister's side
  Rase up an' cried alood—
" Come, come, bairns, this is nae place for you,
  Rin awa' hame oot o' the crood."

But the Maister said, as they turned awa',
  " Let the wee bairns come tae Me!"
An' He gaithered them roun' Him whar He sat,
  An' liftit ane up on His knee.

Ay, He gaithered them roun' Him whar He sat,
  An' straikit their curly hair,
An' He said tae the won'erin' fisher fowk
  That croodit aroun' Him there—

"Send na the weans awa' frae Me,
  But raither this lesson learn—
That nane'll win in at heaven's yett
  That isna as pure as a bairn."

An' He that has ta'en us for kith and kin,
  Tho' a' Prince o' the Far Awa',
Gaithered the wee anes in His airms,
  An' blessed them ane an' a'.

* * * * *

O Thou who watchest the ways o' men,
  Keep oor feet in the heavenly airt,
An' bring us at last tae Thy hame abune,
  As pure as the bairns in he'rt.

PEARL FISHING.

CHAPTER XXIV.

Precious Pearl.

WHEN the Society of Christian Endeavour was started in Oodooville, a little boy who lived near the church was attracted by the singing, and always attended the meetings. When others were joining the society he came forward and said he wanted to join. He was a very little fellow, and his two front teeth were fallen out, so that he spoke with a lisp. His head was all shaven except a little round place on the top, where the hair that was left was tied up in a knot. He wore a yard of cloth about his loins and that was all. This little half-naked person, with his head only a little higher than the table, begged to join the society. He was from a heathen family. My first thought was that he was too young, and did not know what he was asking, but when I.

told him so, tears began to gather in his eyes. He did not know how to pray, so one of the "Look-out Committee" promised to teach him. He said he could read, but had no Bible portion. I told him he must buy one. The next day, to my surprise, he came bringing some vegetables with which to buy a Tamil Gospel of Matthew.

At the next meeting of the society he again asked leave to join. He showed his Matthew's Gospel in which, according to our rules, he had read ten verses a day. He had learned and recited the Lord's prayer. He said he would soon be able to pray in his own words like the other children. He begged to join the society. Seeing his earnestness, we did not like to discourage him, and as the "Look-out Committee" favoured it and said they would look after him, we let him join. So he came up proudly and wrote his name, Vidamutthu, in large Tamil letters. His name means "Precious Pearl." At the next meeting he brought in two of his companions.

One evening that week, as I was taking a moonlight walk, I heard a little voice laboriously reading something aloud. I stopped to listen. It was the Sermon on the Mount. I peeped through the hedge and saw a family circle: a father, mother, and four children, all listening, and this little seven-year-old Vidamutthu reading aloud by the aid of a dim native lamp. I thought of Jesus taking a little child and setting him in the midst. After reading, he sang the verse of the Christian lyric taught in the day-schools that week, and then he prayed a little prayer and at its close recited the Lord's prayer. I stood listening without, and all the family sat quietly listening within. The next Sabbath his mother came to church. I had often before asked her to come, and so had our Christian women, but she had always refused. After church a Christian woman brought her to the inquirers' meeting. I asked her what had led her to come to church. She said that her little son had begged her so hard to come that she could not resist, that he prayed for her every night, and that she had decided to be a Christian. Since then she has come regularly to church. This is the story of how one little "pearl" has begun to reflect Jesus.

There are pearl fisheries off the coast of Ceylon. They are a Government monopoly, and nobody can fish for pearls except those appointed by Government. But there is another kind of fishery in Ceylon, in which all are free to engage. It belongs to Him who said, "Follow Me, and I will make you fishers of men," and every little boy and girl in the home and who gives and prays for Ceylon has a share in this pearl fishery, and can gather gems for the Saviour's crown.

CHAPTER XXV.

MEENATCHIE, THE ISLAND GIRL.

WHEN my sister made a tour among the islands west of Jaffna she found a very bright little girl named Meenatchie, about twelve years of age, who had been studying in a heathen school and had learned to read, but who had never heard of Christ. She asked the parents to allow this little girl to be educated in the Oodooville Girls' Boarding-school, and they consented.

MEENATCHIE (SEATED) AND HER FRIEND.

There is a custom in this school that, when a new class is received, each of the older girls who have been pupils in the school for two or three years selects a girl from the new class as one for whom she will specially care; and the older girl "mothers" the little new girl, caring for her comfort, instructing her in the ways of the school, and above all reading a portion of the Bible with her morning and evening, and teaching her to pray. There is a row of small rooms called "prayer-rooms" built off from the school, into which the girls can go and be quite alone for private prayers as often as they wish. When the new class was received into the school, one of the elder girls chose Meenatchie as her special charge, and began to teach her the wonderful stories of God's love for us, of a Saviour who died for us, and of a heavenly home. These were all new stories to the little girl. After a few days she came to us saying, "The other girls have Bibles of their own,

I have no Bible. My father did not give me a Bible with my other books; what shall I do?" We gave her a copy of one of the gospels in Tamil. A gospel costs just a penny: you see what a penny will do if dropped into the collection-box by some child in England or America. It will give a gospel of Matthew or Mark or Luke or John, in the native language, to some boy or girl in India or Ceylon. A *gospel*, telling the whole story of the life of Christ and the words of Christ. Is it not a good use to make of a penny?

We told Meenatchie that when she had read this gospel through, and could tell something of what it said, we would give her a New Testament. We noticed her afterwards diligently reading it aloud to herself out of school-hours. A few days later she came to us, saying, "I have no hymn-book of my own, and I do wish I had one, so that I might learn to sing these beautiful hymns." We gave her a little book containing twenty-four Christian hymns in the Tamil language. This also costs just a penny. The next morning, when we sang the opening hymn, Meenatchie found it in her new hymn-book, and began to sing with the others at the *top of her voice*, though she did not in the least know the tune: such was her eagerness to learn. I told her she must sing softly and listen to the others. She did this, and having naturally a good ear for music, she soon learned to sing very well and became a member of our school choir.

A weekly prayer-meeting for members of the boarding-school is held on Friday afternoons. At the first prayer-meeting in the new term there was much interest manifested. The older girls felt the great responsibility which rested upon them with regard to the younger ones, many of whom had come from heathen homes, and had not yet given their hearts to Christ. Some of the younger girls had begun to see their need of a Saviour, and many earnest prayers were offered. At the close of the meeting, I said, "Are there not some here who would like to give their hearts to Christ to-day? If so, will they not come to my room, and we will spend a little further time in prayer?" At once little Meenatchie came to my side, and, slipping her hand into mine, said, "Amma, I'll come." Others followed her example, and more than thirty girls came to my room; many prayed with tears for themselves, and for the conversion of their heathen parents and relatives. It moved me strangely that those who had just begun to know a little of Christ's love themselves were longing so intensely that their parents, brothers, and sisters should know it too. We continued to have a second meeting for inquirers after the first for some time, and I think these meetings were blessed to the girls. Day by day, as we taught Meenatchie, it seemed to us that her heart was opening to the truth, just as a flower opens to the sunlight.

After Meenatchie had been in the school a month, her father came from the islands to see her. As she saw him coming in at the gate she ran from the playground to meet him, and my sister, who was standing near, heard her say to him, "I am so glad to see you, O father; I want you to become a Christian." This new-found light and joy was in her little heart, and she never thought of keeping it all to herself: she wanted her father to possess it too. She had only known of Christ one month, but already her heart had come in some measure into harmony with the great loving heart of Him who said, "*Other sheep I have which are not of this fold, them also I must bring.*"

When Meenatchie had been two months in the school, the Sacrament of the Lord's Supper was celebrated one Sabbath in the church, and some of the older girls of the school were among the number received into the church-fold on profession of faith. Meenatchie had never seen a Communion Service before. It was all new to her. At its close she came to us and said, "Please tell me what they were doing in the church to-day." We explained that we were commemorating Christ's death, because He had asked those who loved Him to do so in remembrance of Him. She said eagerly, "Amma, may I join with the others next time?" She loved Christ, and when she learned that He had told us to do this, her little heart responded "yes" to His call; so she said, "May I join next time?" We told her she might join the candidates' class first of all, which she did.

At the end of three months a brief vacation was given to the school, and before dismissing the girls, my sister told them she hoped that during the vacation they would all attend the Sabbath services in their various villages with their parents, and that she hoped they would all try to be present at the great Annual Meeting of the mission, which was to be held at Batticotta. In giving these injunctions she did not think of them being carried out by Meenatchie, as her parents were Hindoos, and attended neither the Sabbath services nor the Annual Meetings. But Meenatchie never thought my sister meant her remarks for others, she was so busy taking them all home to herself.

On going to her island home she took her Tamil gospel and hymn-book, and the first evening, after the family had eaten their evening meal of rice and curry, and were all seated on the veranda enjoying the quiet and bright moonlight and resting after the labours of the day, Meenatchie said, "When I was in the school, I learned to sing some sweet songs. May I sing them now?" They readily assented, for the Tamil people are all very fond of singing. Then the little girl sang from memory several of the beautiful Christian hymns which she had learned. After this she said, "In the school I read some good stories out of a book. May I read some of them to you now?" They assented, as Tamil people are always very fond of stories, and often at this, the resting-time of the day, amuse each other by telling stories and riddles. Meenatchie lighted the little lamp, which is of the simplest construction—a small earthen vessel with oil and a bit of twisted cloth for a wick, and read to them from her little gospel the story of the birth of Christ. Then she said, "I learned to pray to the true Lord in the school, may I pray now?" There was a dead silence in the family circle, as all were worshippers of idols. But the brave little girl knelt down and prayed aloud a simple childlike prayer, asking the true God for Christ's sake to forgive her sins and help her to do right, and bless her dear grandmother and father and mother and brothers and sisters, and help them all to know Him and love Him. This she did night after night all through her vacation, reading, singing, praying aloud, leading the family devotions by the light of a little flickering lamp—herself a little lamp struggling to shine for Jesus in the gloom.

When the Sabbath came she said to her father, "The Ammas told me that I must go to the church on the Sabbath, father; please take me to the church." But the father said, "No, daughter, I cannot take you to the church; I worship Pulliar, and Vedavan, and Kanther Swami, and Siva. If I went to the Christian church all the neighbours would laugh at me and say I had become a Christian." But she said, "Oh, *please*, father, take me to the church, for I *promised the Amma* that I would go to the church;" and she began to weep so bitterly that she was unable to eat her breakfast. When her father saw this his heart was touched, for you must know that the fathers' hearts in Ceylon are just about as soft as the fathers' hearts in England or America, and they love their children just as well, and are as ready to make sacrifices for them. So the father said, "Do not cry, my little daughter; I will go with you this one time." He went, and heard the singing, the reading, the prayers, the addresses by the native Christian catechist, noted the quiet, reverent behaviour, and had no fault to find; so at the invitation of the catechist he came again the next Sabbath.

When my sister and I went on the day appointed to the Annual Meeting at Batticotta, who did we see, to our astonishment, standing in the doorway of the church, but the little Meenatchie with her father on one side of her and her mother on the other, her face radiant with joy as she said to us, "Amma, I've brought them." And so she had; yielding to her daily entreaties, they had come across the water in a small boat, and then a good many miles on foot, and the loving earnestness of a little child had been the motive power. They enjoyed the Annual Meeting, and were much impressed by the services, and by the large orderly assemblage of native Christians—a striking contrast to the noisy crowd which surrounds the heathen temples on festival occasions. When the new term commenced the father and mother both came, bringing Meenatchie back to the school, and they brought a sheep and a bottle of melted butter as a present, saying that their daughter had improved very much while in the school and had been a good girl in the vacation, and they wished to express their thanks to us. We earnestly begged the father and mother to attend the Christian church on their island, and they promised to do so.

Meenatchie was received into the Christian church before the end of the year. It is not the custom to receive those who come from heathen homes until they have been in the school a longer time, but an exception was made in the case of Meenatchie, as all her teachers and the native pastor and the church committee felt convinced that she was truly a converted child, and that in her daily life she was trying to serve Christ.

A TOWER OF THE TEMPLE OF THE GODDESS MEENATCHIE.

I shall never forget the look of joy on her face, or the shining in her large, beautiful black eyes, as she stood up to be received with others into the visible church. Did the "Father of lights" see the shining too, and rejoice with His child? The joy of that day, and of others like it, a hundred-fold more than repaid us for any little sacrifices we may have made in going to the mission-field.

When Meenatchie was baptized she took the English name, Clara Kimball, and dropped the name Meenatchie, which is the name of a heathen goddess, whose great temple stands in Madura. Little Clara still studies in the Boarding-school, and we hope that when she graduates she may go back to her island home, followed by your prayers, to be a blessing to her own people.

THE COBRA.

Strong drink a more deadly foe to India. "At last it biteth like a serpent and stingeth like an adder."

CHAPTER XXVI.

The Liquor Traffic a Great Foe of Missions.

WE found the liquor traffic, authorized and licensed by the British Government, a great foe to Christian work in North Ceylon. The voices of Rachels weeping for their children and refusing to be comforted fell on our ears and aroused our hearts. Broken-hearted wives and mothers, whose husbands or sons had fallen through the drink curse, asked us *why such temptations were placed in their midst? were these always to continue? must they suffer them?* The Government certainly does not dream of the bitterness, of the sorrow and despair with which many of the natives look upon this absolutely ruinous traffic, thrust upon them against their wishes for the sake of a revenue. In India and Ceylon the liquor traffic is purely *a Government monopoly.* The right to sell liquor in a district is sold at public auction to the highest bidder. When some one has bought the right and promised to give the Government a large sum of money for the same, he does not wish to be a loser by the transaction, so he opens as many liquor shops as possible in the district. These are located in the towns and villages near the tea and cinchona estates, in the mining districts, and on the roadsides along which there is most travel, and by means of these multiplied places of temptation "a nation of abstainers is fast becoming a nation of drunkards."

The religions of the Hindus, Mohammedans, and Buddhists forbid the use of strong drink, and formerly the people of India and Ceylon were for the most part total abstainers. Formerly spirits were high-priced and hard to get, and drunkenness was uncommon because there was little temptation to drink. But in any country it the facilities for obtaining strong drink are increased the consumption is increased: if the facilities for obtaining strong drink are diminished the consumption is diminished. In India and Ceylon the facilities for obtaining strong drink have been abnormally increased. The British Government for the sake of a revenue has made strong drink to be cheap and plentiful. In Ceylon nine times as much is spent for strong

8*

drink as is expended by the Government for education. In Bengal, where the "outstill" system prevails, "Bhuli" is sold for four annas and less per quart bottle. In that province the excise revenue has in ten years increased twenty-nine lakhs of rupees. In Assam the excise revenue has *trebled* in ten years. In the North-West Provinces the excise revenue has more than *doubled* in ten years. In the whole of India the excise revenue has increased in thirteen years *seventy-five per cent!*

Archdeacon Farrar said in a recent address, "It is now a considerable time ago that an Archdeacon of Bombay, with whom I was acquainted, gave the shocking testimony in public that for every Christian whom we (Great Britain) had made in India we had made 100 drunkards." What do these figures mean? They mean that tens of thousands and hundred of thousands of people in India, who formerly were total abstainers, have fallen before the multiplied temptations placed before them. Is this to be wondered at? If men and women in Great Britain and America, with centuries of civilization behind them, with Christian influences all around them, cannot withstand the temptation of the open public-house and liquor saloon, how could it be hoped that the poor ignorant people of India could withstand such temptations? Is it not a *shame* to place such temptations in the presence of heathen peoples? It is the glory of the strong to protect the weak. Should not the great British nation protect rather than tempt its subject races? It is the province of Government to make it easy to do right and hard to do wrong, but in India in the matter of this liquor traffic Government has done just the reverse.

It has been said by a great English statesman in the House of Commons that "the combined evils of war and pestilence and famine are not so great as those evils which flow from strong drink;" and it has been estimated that eighty-four per cent. of the crime is caused either directly or indirectly by strong drink. If this be so, has not poor India crime enough of its own, sorrow and poverty enough of its own, without having this, the curse of Great Britain, imported into India and fostered there against the wishes of the people, for the sake of a revenue? Another of England's great statesmen has said, "Gentlemen, I refuse to consider a question of revenue alongside of a question of morals," and he has said again, "Give me sober and industrious people, and I will soon show you where to get a revenue."

The Government in India for the sake of a revenue creates a class of men whose business it is to push the traffic in strong drink. Surely a revenue should be paid by men who are able to pay it. We should not tempt men to give up their purity and allow their homes to be destroyed for the sake of a revenue. Some one has said, "I feel less shame for the savage who, with rude conscience and untaught life, turns cannibal and picks the bones of human beings that he may live, than for those who stand up and plead that this traffic may exist which shall take the money out of the pockets of the poor, and destroy hearts and homes, in order that their own taxation may be lessened."

Sometimes it is said by Englishmen when speaking of India and Ceylon, "It is true that the liquor shops are there, but the natives are not forced to drink." Yet we cannot help feeling that a great wrong is being done, because those ignorant people are being *tempted.* *Is it right to tempt?* The devil does not force people to do wrong, he only *tempts*, yet the *devil is the devil because his business is to tempt.*

We were grieved to find that intemperance was spreading among the people in North Ceylon, that many were using country-made and imported liquors, that many families were in great sorrow because a husband, or son, or brother, having gone to some of the large towns in Ceylon or India and adopted the drinking customs now prevailing in those towns, had learned to drink. We frequently heard the most pitiful tales from weeping wives and mothers in many villages around us. We began to hold temperance meetings among our people. In so doing we felt a lack of temperance literature in the native language; we had a little book of thirty-seven temperance hymns prepared in the Tamil language, and 5,000 copies of this book printed. We wished to have temperance tracts to circulate among the people; we therefore had several of John B. Gough's temperance lectures translated, and circulated in Ceylon a few thousand copies which had been printed in our mission press. But as Tamil is spoken by sixteen millions of people in Southern India, and as we knew that drinking habits were spreading there, and in all parts of India as well, we wished that these temperance lectures might be circulated among these millions, so that they might not drink blindly, but might know what ruin and degradation would follow. We therefore made arrangements with each of the five great Tract Societies of India to have these lectures, in whole or in part, translated and published by them in six or seven of the leading languages of India. The Madras Tract Society has also agreed to publish a temperance catechism of 137 questions and answers which we had had prepared in the Tamil language.

We held many temperance meetings in our district, and at

A WAYSIDE INN.

these meetings over 1400 pledges were taken. But although we have worked earnestly for this cause, we feel as if *while we have been trying to rescue one drunkard the liquor shops have been making ten.* The petition of the World's Women's Christian Temperance Union was sent to us for circulation. We had it translated into Tamil and Singalese and circulated in those languages, and in English, circulating at the same time a somewhat similar petition to be signed by men. We sent these petitions to various missionaries in Ceylon, who gave them into the hands of their native pastors, catechists, teachers, and Bible-women, and they were thus circulated by responsible parties. The natives in general expressed great eagerness to sign the petitions. We were told that many Hindus signed these petitions with a prayer. Raising their hands and eyes to heaven, they would say, "Thervan ethu say-ert-thume," i.e. "May the Lord prosper this." In traversing India in 1886 we had this petition translated and circulated in ten of the leading Indian languages through the medium of the five great Religious Tract Societies of India. We secured from India and Ceylon over 33,000 signatures to these petitions. These have been forwarded to the secretary of the World's Women's Christian Temperance Union. We also secured the insertion of temperance articles in many of the leading newspapers of India, and we had the opportunity of seeing much of mission work, and of addressing various assemblies, mission schools, &c., during our visit. We have great pleasure in stating that throughout this tour, in which we met over 200 missionaries and were entertained in many mission homes, we never saw a drop of strong drink on any missionary's table; and we found many missionaries to be earnest temperance workers, having total abstinence societies in their churches and schools. We pray that the day may come soon when *every foreign missionary* may be a *pledged total abstainer.* We believe these petitions voiced the real desire of the people, viz. the entire abolition of the traffic. They wonder that the British Government is willing to take a revenue from such a source; they remind us that their Hindu and Mohammedan rulers did not take a revenue from the sale of intoxicating drinks, but instead forbade the sale, and they suggest that Indian seas and Indian soil furnish better sources for obtaining a revenue than the liquor traffic; they would ask the Christians of Great Britain, who have sent them the Scriptures in which they are taught to pray, "Lead us not into temptation," that this *great temptation* may be removed from them. Can nothing be done to give the people a voice in this matter which so closely affects their homes? If the natives of Ceylon and India had local option in regard to this matter, they would, we believe, very quickly shut up these liquor shops.

Surgeon-Major R. Pringle, M.D., of Her Majesty's Bengal Army, after thirty years experience in India says, "I can speak for ten millions in the North-West Provinces, when I state that, if local self-government were granted, not a grog-shop would remain in twelve months; the Mohammedans would not soil their fingers with rupees gathered by 'shame-water,' and the Hindu would gladly avail himself of the opportunity of showing his contempt for and disgust with the co-religionist whose thirst for silver was so great that he bought at a public auction the privilege to sell the Government 'shame-water.'"

A native of India, Nâuda Lal Ghosh, a Barrister-at-Law, says: "The temperance question is not only a question of morality, but also an economical question. About *forty millions* of people in India do not have enough of food from year's end to year's end, and when this poison of drink is spreading among them, what will be the economical condition of India? We have statistics, and know well that the people are in abject poverty, and yet there comes the demon of drink to intensify their misery, introduced by a Christian Government. I do not wish to blame the Government too much, but I hold it is the duty of all Englishmen, who hold the destiny of two hundred and fifty millions of their fellow-subjects in their hands, to stop the current of that poison, and to give to India true moral teaching instead. I appeal to you to abolish the poison of drink. We have municipal institutions on the elective and nominative basis, and I think it is high time the Government took the matter into serious consideration and allowed *local option* instead of selling licences to the highest bidder."

Is the liquor traffic to be allowed to entrench itself in India? Is a curse to come to India through this traffic similar to that which has come to China through the opium traffic forced upon her by the British Government? There are those who say that the amount of strong drink consumed in India in proportion to the population is small *as yet.* Perhaps it is, but it is *a growing evil*, and this is surely cause for the gravest concern. When the opium traffic was begun with China, the amount sent from India was 200 cases, and though some protested against the traffic, the public conscience of Great Britain was lulled to sleep by being told "two hundred cases is a small amount. The traffic is a little thing." But can we ever say of any *evil* "It is a little thing"? Now the amount sent annually from India to China is not merely 200 cases, but 85,000 cases, containing over 5,000 *tons of opium!* All this is exported from India, and sent to debauch the Chinese. The British Government is responsible for this traffic, since the opium in India is a monopoly of the Government, from which it derives a revenue of over £5,000,000 annually. It has been said by the missionaries in China that if the people of England could see for one hour the poverty and wretchedness, the ruin and death caused in China by the use of opium, they would be horrified. What notion of the justice of Him who rules the world must he have who supposes that a nation can commit such exceeding wickedness and yet escape retribution? "Be not deceived: God is not mocked, for whatsoever a man (or nation) soweth, that shall he also reap." There is no power on earth can escape from this sentence. Returned missionaries from China tell us that this traffic is "one huge ministry of vice," and is one of the greatest obstacles to the evangelization of China. When the poor opium victim, to satisfy his fearful craving, has sold one article after another, till all his property is gone, he will, in many instances, sell his children into servitude and his wife into a life of shame. Missionaries have told us how, powerless to interfere, they have stood outside of Chinese homes in the dead of night, and heard the screams of women and girls who were being sold by a husband or father into a life worse than death, because the opium-smoker must have money with which to buy the drug. To-day, while we sit in our comfortable homes, there are tens of thousands of families in China suffering unspeakable misery on account of Great Britain's dealing with that nation in this matter. When one of the missionaries in China was preaching to a company in the open-air, and speaking about hell, one in the crowd replied, "Yes, we know about hell; since England sent us the opium China has become a hell." On another occasion, when a missionary was urging some Chinese hearers to accept Christ, one old woman said, "Was it not your country that sent us the opium? Well, we don't want your opium, and we don't want your Christ." Oh! what a blot is thus put upon that Name which is above every name, because a so-called Christian nation engages in this accursed and soul-destroying traffic! The Rev. J. Hudson Taylor, Director of the China Inland Mission, at the great Missionary Conference held in London in 1888, said, "When we look back to eighty years of missionary labour in China, and compare it with the results of eighty years of commmercial labour, I am afraid our brows must be covered with shame and our hearts filled with sorrow. After eighty years of missionary labour we are thankful for thirty-two thousand communicants. After eighty years of commercial labour there are one hundred and fifty millions of the Chinese who are either personally smokers of the opium or sufferers by the opium vice of husband or wife, father or mother, or some relative. You may go through China, and you will find thousands—I can safely say tens of thousands—of towns and villages in which there are but small traces of the Bible or of Christian influence. You will scarcely find a hamlet in which the opium-pipe does not reign. Ah! we have given China something besides the Gospel; something that is doing more harm in a week than the united efforts of all our Christian Missionaries are doing good in a year. Oh, the evils of opium! The slave trade was bad; the drink is bad; the licensing of vice is bad; but the opium traffic is

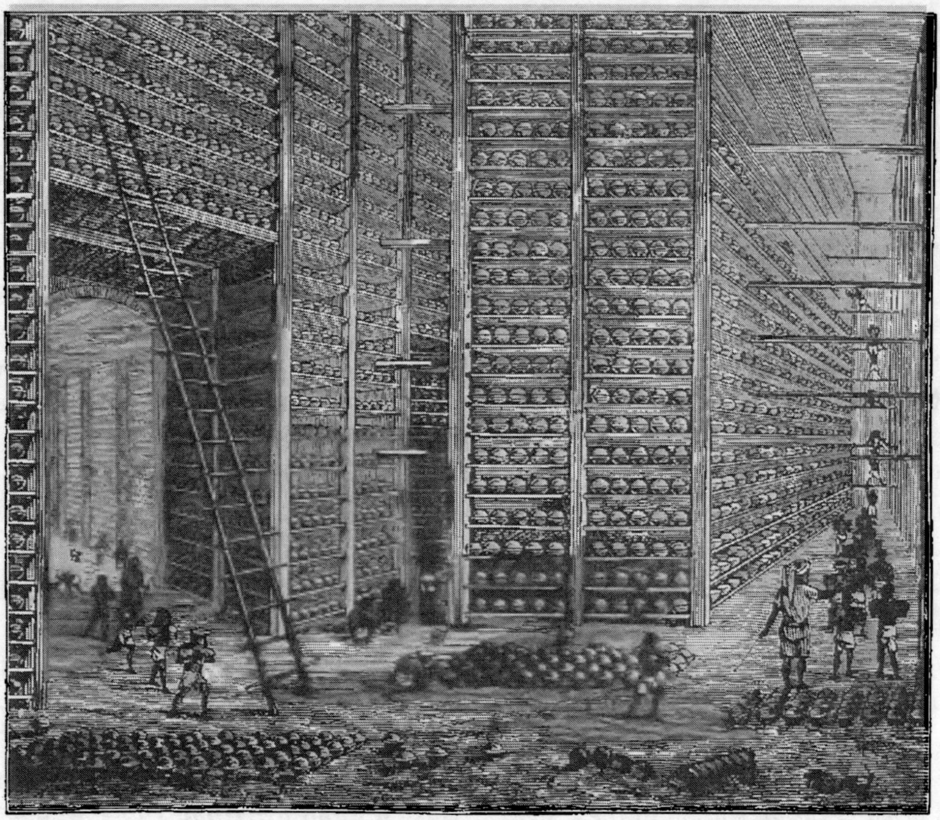

THE STACKING ROOM IN THE GOVERNMENT OPIUM FACTORY AT PATNA.

the sum of all villanies. It debauches more families than drink, it makes more slaves directly than the slave trade, and it demoralizes more lives than all the licensing systems in the world. Will you not pray, my friends? I entreat you to pray to the mighty God that He will bring this great evil to an end. The common reason brought forward in extenuation of the traffic is this:—'England cannot afford to do right.' Now, I would say, England cannot afford to do wrong. Nay, you must not do one wrong thing to escape another. It is said you must not starve India in order to deliver China. My dear friends, it is always right to do right, and the God in heaven, who is the great Governor of the Universe, never created this world on such lines that the only way to properly govern India was to curse China. There is no curse in God's government. The Indian Government has taken this ground—that it has the right to prevent the production of opium, except at the Government factories. Let it add to this, that it shall not be produced at the Government factories, and we ask no more."

The late Earl of Shaftesbury well said, "Let every missionary, and every lay agent, and every woman, and every child, refrain from being silent upon that question" (the opium question). Henry Richards on one occasion used these words:—"I am not ashamed to say that I am one of those who believe that there is a God who ruleth in the kingdom of men, and that it is not safe for a community, any more than an individual, recklessly and habitually to affront those great principles of truth, and justice, and humanity, on which, I believe, He governs the world. And we may be quite sure of this, that, in spite of our pride of place and power, in spite of our vast possessions and enormous resources, in spite of our boasted forces by land and sea—if we come into conflict with that Power we shall be crushed like an egg-shell against a granite rock."

This opium traffic between India and China, for which the British Government is responsible, is a great national sin, and, if unrepented of, will surely be followed by national judgment, for the government of God is just, the government of God is retributive, and if God calls Great Britain to an account, will He not call *every man and woman in Great Britain* to an account? For the nation is made up of individuals, and will He not hold each one responsible—not only for what they are doing, but for *all they might do?* What makes it possible for these great evils—the liquor traffic in India and the opium traffic with China—to exist under British rule? *Public sentiment in Great Britain makes it possible.* The British Government is a government by the people; therefore these great evils exist because the people of Great Britain are willing that they should exist, and the work to be done by those who love India, and China, and Great Britain herself, is to arouse a *Christian public sentiment* in Britain which shall *demand the overthrow* of these evils. Have not the *Christian Churches* of Britain the power, if they were thoroughly awake and in earnest, to create a public sentiment which would demand of Parliament, in the name of God and of humanity, that these two great iniquities should be prohibited? *They have the power*, and if these evils go on in the future it will not be because the Churches of Great Britain *could not* stop them, but because these churches were asleep, and *would not* stop them, and God will hold the Churches responsible for the continuation of these evils.

Some one asked the venerable Dr. Beecher, "How long must the liquor traffic continue?" His reply was, "*Just as long as the Christian Churches are willing that it should, and not a day longer.*" "The measure of our *ability* is the measure of our *responsibility*." Not to protest against this evil—not to act—is to acquiesce, and that is complicity with the evil. "To him that knoweth to do good and doeth it not, to him it is SIN." We are accustomed to think that at the last day we shall be judged on account of what we have done. Perhaps we shall rather be judged for what we have failed to do. Christ has told us He will say to some at that day, "I was an hungred, and ye gave Me *no meat;* I was thirsty, and ye gave Me *no drink;* I was a stranger, and ye *took Me not in*; naked, and ye *clothed Me not*; sick, and in prison, and ye *visited Me not. Inasmuch as ye did it* NOT *to one of the* LEAST OF THESE, *ye did it* NOT TO ME."

Look at the magnitude of the evil of the liquor traffic. See, for example, what is going on in Africa. It has been said that for one missionary sent to Africa to evangelize its heathen tribes there are sent 70,000 barrels of rum for purposes of barter. It was stated in the *Church Missionary Intelligencer* that on 250 miles of coast-line in the tropical region of Africa—on the west coast—no less than twenty ships a year arrive there, with, on an average, a thousand tons of intoxicating drink on each of them. Think of it—*twenty thousand tons* of intoxicating drink every year poured in on that limited tract of country! One of the missionaries connected with the Church Missionary Society says, "If this thing is continued, it is only a question of a few years for me and my people." Sir Richard Burton, the great African traveller, writes, "It is my sincere belief that *if the slave trade were revived, with all its horrors, and Africa could get rid of the white man, with the gunpowder and rum which he has introduced, Africa would be a gainer in happiness by the exchange.*" Sir Charles Warren, late Commissioner to South Africa, has said, "*The blood of thousands of natives is at the present time crying to heaven against the British race*, and yet, from motives of expediency, we refuse to take any action."

From a memorial sent out by the World's Women's Christian Temperance Union the following statement is made:—"It is a fully authenticated fact that, through the operation of a few merchants and trading companies in America, Germany, Holland, England, France, and Portugal, a flood of deadly, intoxicating liquor is being poured into the Congo Free State and the Basin of the Niger. During the year 1885 (the last year for which we have full statistics) more than *ten million gallons* of the cheapest and vilest spirits ever manufactured were sent from these *six Christian countries* to the ignorant savages of Africa." Mrs. Mary C. Hind, speaking on the subject of this memorial before the great Missionary Conference held in London in 1888, said:—"We have been trying to keep the Atlantic back with a broom too many years. We want to get at the great basal truth, *prohibition*, so that the liquor does not go to these parts. This memorial is sent out by the W.C.T.U. of the World. They have nothing to do with any other parish than the world. Beloved, it is too late in the day for us to do anything else than sound the note of prohibition. And as to the matter of revenue, God forbid I should mention it. *It is a burning shame to our Christian nations to talk about a revenue that comes from the blood, and tears, and cries, and groans, and moans, and the damnation of thousands of precious souls.*"

Is it *nothing* to us that whole nations are being demoralized by this iniquitous traffic? If some one were to tempt and ruin *your* sons and daughters, you would *feel* it, but these are *the sons and daughters of the Living God.* He made them. He cares for them. He gave His Son for their redemption. Will He not call professing Christians to account for their negligence and indifference towards this evil, which is causing the ruin of millions for whom Christ died? Paul says:—"*To the weak became I as weak, that I might gain the weak. I am made all things to all men, that I might by all means save some.*" And he admonishes us:—"*We, then, that are strong ought to bear the infirmities of the weak, and not to please ourselves. For even Christ pleased not Himself.*" Remembering the *great* sacrifice which He made for us, would that those everywhere who profess His name might make the little sacrifice of banishing strong drink as a beverage from their tables and homes, and give the influence of their *example*, as well as their *prayers* and most earnest *efforts*, to the overthrowing of the great evil which is ruining so many millions of mankind. When Christ our Lord and Master was on this earth, He gave us the great command:—"*Thou shalt love the Lord thy God with all thine heart, and thy neighbour as thyself.*" Love will not sit idly down in despair. Be the task never so gigantic, "love will find out a way."

Clarkson, in contemplating the horrors of the slave trade, said to himself that "if these things were true, it was time that somebody should see these calamities to an end," and forthwith he went to work, with heart and soul and mind on fire, with an energy that never tired, and faith that never faltered, till God crowned his Herculean efforts with success. He had to work in the face of fierce opposition. Cool-headed and cool-hearted men pronounced against the enterprise. Boswell, in his "Life of Johnson," said that "to abolish the slave trade would be to shut the gates of mercy on mankind." We are told by Mrs. Harriet Beecher Stowe, in her "Sunny Memories," that, "As usual, the cause of oppression was defended by the most impudent lying. The slave trade was asserted to be the latest revised edition of philanthropy."

It was said that the poor African—the slave of miserable oppression in his own country—was wafted by it to an asylum in a Christian land; that the middle passage was to the poor negro a perfect elysium, infinitely happier than anything he had ever known in his own country. All this was said while manacles, and handcuffs, and thumbscrews, and instruments to force open the mouth, were a regular part of the stock for a slave-ship, and were hanging in the shop windows of Liverpool for sale. It was perfectly well known that in very many cases slave traders made direct incursions into the country, kidnapped and carried off the inhabitants of whole villages, but the question was, how to prove it. A gentleman whom Clarkson accidentally met on one of his journeys informed him that he had been in company about a year before with a sailor—a very respectable-looking young man—who had actually been engaged in one of these expeditions. He had spent half an hour with him at an inn. He described his person, but knew nothing of his name or place of abode. All that he knew was that he belonged to a ship of war in ordinary, but knew nothing of the post. Clarkson determined that this man should be produced as a witness, and knew no better way than to go personally to all the ships in ordinary until the individual was found. He actually visited every seaport town, and boarded every ship, till, in the very *last* port and in the very *last* ship which remained, the individual was found, and found to be possessed of just the facts and information which were necessary. For seven years Clarkson maintained a correspondence with 400 persons with his own hand. He annually wrote a book on behalf of the cause. In that time he had travelled more than 35,000 miles in search of evidence. By the labours of Clarkson and his companions an incredible excitement was produced throughout all England. Pictures and models of slave-ships, accounts of the cruelties practised in the trade, were circulated *with an industry which left not a man, or woman, or child in England uninstructed.* After the committee had published the facts and sent them to every town in England, Clarkson followed them up by journeying to all the places to see that they were read and attended to. Of the state of feeling at this time Clarkson writes:—"First, I may observe that there was no town through which I passed in which there was not some one individual who had left off the use of sugar. In the smaller towns there were from ten to fifty by estimation, and in the larger from 200 to 500 who made this sacrifice to virtue. These were of all ranks and parties. Rich and poor, Churchmen and Dissenters, had adopted the measure. Even grocers had left off trading in the article in some places. In gentlemen's families where the master had set the example the servants had often voluntarily followed it, and even children who were capable of understanding the history of the sufferings of the Africans excluded, with the most virtuous resolution, the sweets to which they had been accustomed from their lips. By the best computation I was able to make from notes taken down in my journey, no fewer than 300,000 persons had abandoned the use of sugar." It was the *reality, depth, and earnestness of the public feeling thus roused which pressed with resistless force upon the Government*, for the Government of England yields to popular demands quite as readily as that of America. After years of protracted struggle, the victory was at last won. The slave trade was finally abolished throughout the British Empire. At this time the religious mind and conscience of England gained through this very struggle a power which it has never lost. The principle adopted by them was the same so sublimely adopted by the

Church in America with reference to the foreign missionary cause: "The field is the world!" Shall not those who love the Lord Jesus Christ and care for the welfare of their fellow-men, encouraged by the example of such heroic toilers as Clarkson, *work with like self-denying earnestness, unwavering faith, and whole-hearted devotion* toward the emancipation of their brothers and sisters, *all the world around*, from a more fearful slavery, the slavery of strong drink and opium, by the entire abolition of these traffics? We believe in the possible and final overthrow of these traffics, just because we believe in *God*. We have the glorious promise that one day "the earth shall be full of the knowledge of the Lord, as the waters cover the sea." Let us work in hope, because, "if God be for us, who can be against us?" Though few in numbers, we are not in the minority; we are in the majority, for "one with God is a majority."

> "History's pages but record
> One death-grapple in the darkness,
> 'Twixt old systems and the Word.
> Truth for ever on the scaffold—
> Wrong for ever on the throne.
> Yet that scaffold sways the future,
> And behind the dim unknown
> Standeth *God* within the shadow,
> Keeping watch above His own."

If He is but watching over us and caring for the cause so dear to us, then we can labour on in boundless hope, knowing that the truth and the right are sure to prevail. "He shall not fail nor be discouraged till He have set judgment in the earth." Christ taught His disciples to pray, "Thy kingdom come; Thy will be done on earth as it is in heaven." All down the ages men and women have been praying that prayer. Would Christ have taught us to pray that prayer if He had never intended to answer it? Surely He is the hearer and *answerer* of prayer. Surely He means to answer that prayer, and the time will come when men on earth will do His will according to their measure, as the angels do it in heaven. One day the glorious vision foreseen by the beloved disciple shall be realized. "The kingdoms of this world are become the kingdoms of our Lord and of His Christ, and He shall reign for ever and ever." (Rev. xi. 15.) Those who in Christ's name and for His sake are working for the ennobling and the purifying of humanity are "labourers together with God," and the victory they fight for is sure.

> "There is no hopeless sorrow;
> Wrong ever builds a tottering throne,
> And Christ shall reign to-morrow."

THE MISSES LEITCH AND A GROUP OF NATIVE CHRISTIANS.

CHAPTER XXVII.

Farewell Address from the Native Christians.

DEAR MISSIONARY FRIENDS,—We are assembled here to trespass a little on your valuable time on the eve of your departure home, and desire to be allowed to give expression to the sentiments of respect and esteem we entertain for you.

Your connection for the past seven years with the American Ceylon Mission, and consequently with the Christians and other residents of Manepy and Panditerippu whom we represent, we are happy to say, has been altogether pleasant and successful in a missionary point of view.

You have always evinced a deep interest both in our spiritual and temporal welfare, and the occasions in which your guidance and advice and prompt help have benefited us have been many. The progress our young men and women especially have made through your efforts in several departments of social Christian life is prized by us highly. The catholic spirit with which you went through your work, and the toleration of views that we noticed in you in all your dealings with us, have been two prominent points of admiration to us. Your presence in the schools where our youths are taught, in our church meetings, improvement societies, youths' associations, &c., have inspired always a new life into them. It may not be amiss to mention that you have made the Christmas-tree a regular institution with the Sunday-school children, Christian and heathen, for whose efficient training in Bible knowledge we are much indebted to you.

Your efforts to spread a taste for Christian music, both vocal and instrumental, in our district, and your work in connection with the temperance movement, and the Endowment Fund of the Oodooville Girls' Boarding-school, will by themselves repay all the sacrifice you made in leaving your home on a missionary enterprise. But it is unnecessary here to mention the numerous ways through which your missionary spirit and social kindness have shone in our midst, and above all the meekness and patience with which you have reflected the life and doings of the Great Master. All these, dear friends, we assure you will ever be remembered by us with heart-felt gratitude and thankfulness.

Although your short absence from our midst will be felt by us, we hope your trip home ("Home, Sweet Home") will eventually prove beneficial to Christian work here, when, in the providence of God, you may return with redoubled energy and health.

We would take this opportunity to tender our compliments to your dear brother, Mr. G. W. Leitch, who had, we are sorry to say, to cut short his work amongst us. At the same time we would send through you our hearty thanks to the Christian churches in America, which have contributed their mites towards Christianizing this land, and ask of them still to continue in their wrestlings for us before the throne of Grace, as the work already accomplished in Jaffna will not bear comparison with the mountains, of Satan's raising, that are yet to be removed.

We also beg you to accept the accompanying presents of two Tamil Bibles, as tokens of remembrance from us. We will not take up more of your time now, but wish you a safe voyage forth and back, and a hearty good-bye.

***

FAREWELL LYRIC No. 1.

(*Translation from the Tamil.*)

1. O gentle ladies, who have come from a distant land;
Who have left relatives and friends for our sake;
Who have come over in ships and boats;
Who have shown us the path to the distant world;
How shall we bear it if you leave us? How shall we bear it?

2. O pious and chaste ladies; O pure treasures;
Who have opened schools in different places;
Who have taught sinners the way of redemption;
How shall we bear it if you leave us? How shall we bear it?

We have prospered by the good done by you?
It is difficult to reward you;
We bless you, O dear jewels;
We have been brought to life;
We will not forget you;
We have come to thank you heartily;
How shall we bear it when you leave us? How shall we bear it?

FAREWELL LYRIC No. 2.

(*Translation from the Tamil.*)

1. O ladies, good mothers,
Good-bye to you.
We prostrate ourselves at your golden feet.
Good-bye to you.

2 Your love did bind us like a cord.
We cannot bear separation,
The moment for which has come.
Good-bye to you.

3. You dealt with us like parents;
You forgave us our faults;
You fed us with knowledge;
We bid you good-bye lovingly;
Good-bye to you.

4. Our spirit trembles, we faint:
We have lost our comfort;
Yet it seems necessary that you should go.
We bid you good-bye lovingly;
Good-bye to you.

THE TRAVELLER'S PALM.

CHAPTER XXVIII.

ELIZA AGNEW, OR ONE WOMAN'S WORK IN THE FOREIGN FIELD.

ONE day the teacher in a day-school in New York City, while giving a lesson in geography, pointed out to her pupils the heathen and the Christian lands, and she must have spoken some very earnest words to them, for then and there a little girl, eight years of age, named Eliza Agnew, resolved that, if it were God's will, she would be a missionary when she grew up, and help to tell the heathen about Jesus. She never forgot this resolve. Until she was thirty years of age she was detained at home, because there were near relations who needed her care. But when she had reached that age, and her dear ones had been called away from earth to heaven, she was free to leave her home, and she went as a missionary to Ceylon.

Some years before this, when the first missionaries reached North Ceylon, they could not find, among the more than 300,000 people there, a single native woman or girl who could read. There were a few men and boys who could read, but the people did not think it worth while to teach the girls. They said, "What are girls good for, excepting to cook food?" &c. "Besides," they said, "girls could not learn to read any more than sheep." The missionaries said to them, "You are mistaken. Girls can learn to read as well as boys." So they opened mission day-schools not only for boys, but for girls also.

Though the parents willingly allowed their sons to attend these schools, they were very unwilling to let their daughters remain long enough to receive an education, as it was common for parents to give their daughters in marriage when they were only ten or twelve years of age. Seeing this, one of the missionary ladies wished to commence a boarding-school for girls. She wished to have the native girls separated from the influences of their heathen homes, and brought under daily Christian influence. But none of the people would send their daughters to her.

One day there were two little girls playing in the flower-garden in front of the missionary's house at Oodooville. Ceylon is in the tropics, only nine degrees north of the equator. In North Ceylon there are two seasons, the "*wet*" and the "*dry.*" The dry season lasts nine months, and during that time there is scarcely any rain; but in the wet season, November, December, and January, it rains nearly every day, and sometimes the rain falls in torrents—between nine and ten inches have been known to fall in twenty-four hours. While these two little girls were playing, there

TAMIL GIRLS IN A BOARDING-SCHOOL.

came on a heavy shower of rain, and as they had not time to go home, they ran for shelter into the missionary's house. It continued to rain all that afternoon and evening, and the little girls became very hungry and began to cry. The missionary lady gave them bread and bananas. The younger girl ate, but the older girl refused to eat. After a time, when the rain ceased a little, the parents went to look for their daughters. They had supposed they would be in some neighbour's house, but found them in that of the missionary. When they heard that the younger one had eaten, they were very angry, for they said, "She has lost caste." They found fault with the missionary lady, and the mother said, "You have given my child food, and it has broken caste and is polluted, and now we shall not be able to arrange a marriage for it. What shall we do? You may take the child and bring it up."

The missionary lady had been wishing for native girls to come to her, whom she might educate in a boarding-school, and here was a mother actually saying she might take her daughter, so the missionary lady thought that perhaps this was the Lord's way of enabling her to start the boarding-school. She took the little girl, fed and clothed her, and began teaching her the 247 letters of the Tamil alphabet. She sprinkled a little sand on the floor of the veranda, and taught the child to write the letters in the sand. By-and-by, some of the playmates of this little girl came to see her, and when they saw her writing the letters in the sand, they thought that this was some kind of new play, and they also wanted to learn. The Tamil children have good memories, and in a very short time they committed to memory the 247 letters of the alphabet, and were able to read. Their parents seeing this, and that the little girl was well cared for and happy, soon began to entrust more of their daughters to the care of the missionary lady. This was the beginning of the Oodooville Girls' Boarding-school, which was, perhaps, the first boarding-school for girls in a heathen land, having been commenced in 1824.

After Miss Agnew went to Ceylon, she became the head of this boarding-school. She remained in Ceylon for forty-three years without once going home for a rest or a change. When friends would ask her, "Are you not going to America for a vacation?" she would always reply, "No; I have no time to do so. I am too busy." Through all those forty-three unbroken years, during which God granted to her remarkable health, she was too busy even to think of going home.

In the Oodooville Girls' Boarding-school she taught the children, and even some of the grandchildren, of her first pupils. More than 1000 girls have studied under her. She was much loved by the girls, who each regarded her as a mother, and she was poetically called by the people, "The mother of a thousand daughters." During the years she taught in the school more than 600 girls went out from it as Christians. We

THREE GENERATIONS.

believe that no girl having taken its whole course has ever graduated as a heathen. Most of these girls came from heathen homes and heathen villages, but in this school they learned of Christ and of His great love, and surrendered their young hearts to Him.

Miss Agnew lived with us in our home the last two years of her life, when she had grown feeble and was no longer able to retain the charge of the boarding-school. We felt her presence in our home to be a daily blessing.

Near the close of her brief illness, and when we knew that she had not many hours to live, one of the missionaries present asked her if he should offer prayer. She eagerly assented. He asked, "Is there anything for which you would like me specially to pray?" She replied, "*Pray for the women of Jaffna, that they may come to Christ.*" She had no thought about herself. All through her missionary life she had thought very little about herself. Her thought was for *the women of Jaffna*, that they might *know Christ;* that they might know that in Him they had an Almighty Saviour, a great burden-bearer, a friend that sticketh closer than a brother, one who had borne their griefs and carried their sorrows and could give their troubled, hungry, sorrowing hearts *His own peace.* At the very time when she was asking prayers for the women of Jaffna, every room in our house was filled with native Christian women who, when girls, had been her pupils, and they were praying for her—that if it were the Lord's will to take her then to Himself, He would save her from suffering and pain. God heard their prayer, and she passed away like one going into a sweet sleep. The attendance at the funeral service was very large. Many native pastors, catechists, teachers, lawyers, Government officials and others, the leading men of Jaffna Peninsula, who had married girls trained in the Oodooville Girls' Boarding-school, came to the funeral service, bringing their wives and children. As we looked over that large audience and saw everywhere faces full of love and eyes full of tears, and knew that to hundreds of homes she had brought the light and hope and joy of the Gospel, we could not help thinking *how precious a life consecrated to Christ may be.*

In hundreds of villages in Ceylon and India there is just such a work waiting to be done by Christian young women as that which, with God's blessing, Miss Agnew accomplished in the Jaffna Peninsula. Heathen lands are open to-day as they have never been open before. The women of heathen lands need the Gospel. The stronghold of heathenism is in the homes. Many of the men in India have to some extent lost faith in their old superstitious creeds, but the women, who are secluded in the homes, cling to the heathen worship. What else can they do? They must cling to something, and the majority of them have not heard of Christ. They are teaching the children to perform the heathen ceremonies, to sing the songs in praise of the heathen gods, and thus they are moulding the habits of thought of the coming generation. Some one has truly said, "If we are to win India for Christ, we must lay our hands on the hands that rock the cradles, and teach Christian songs to the lips that sing the lullabies, and if we can win the *mothers* of India to Christ, her *future sons* will soon be brought to fall at the feet of their Redeemer."

There are in India 120 millions of women and girls. How many lady missionaries are there working among these? In the report of the last Decennial Conference, the number is given as 480, counting those of all Protestant missionary societies. Might not more be sent to that great work? We are told that there are a million more women than men in Great Britain. Could not many of these be spared from their homes, and could not some possessed of private means go on a self-supporting mission to this great field?

Think of the 21 millions of widows in India. What a terrible lot is theirs! They are regarded as under a curse. They are doomed to innumerable hardships. It is deemed meritorious to heap abuse upon them. It is thought the gods are angry with them, and that the death of their husbands is a punishment on them for some sin committed either in this or in some previous life. Their lot is so hard to bear that again and again they have said to the missionaries, "Why did the English Government take from us the right to be burnt on the funeral pyre with our dead husbands? for that were better than what we have to endure." But Christian women could give to these widows of India the Gospel with its message of hope, and before the brightness of its shining the darkness of their despair would flee away. The knowledge of the love of Christ would help them to bear their otherwise intolerable burdens. Let us remember that Christ has told us that whatsoever service we render to the least of His little ones, He will regard it as done to Him, and that whatever we leave undone of that which was in our power to do, He will regard the neglect and slight as shown to Him. *Are there not many in darkness to-day who might have had the Gospel had Christians done what they could for them?*

MOTHER AND BABES.

Failure to realize responsibility does not diminish it. Zenanas which forty years ago were locked and barred are to-day open. Especially is this the case in towns where there are Christian colleges. Wherever the Hindu men have been educated in these mission colleges, they are now willing and even desirous that their wives, daughters, and sisters should be taught. We have been told by Hindu gentlemen, that there are many educated men in India to-day who are convinced of the truth of Christianity, and would confess Christ, were it not that a wife or mother, who has never been instructed about Christ, would bitterly oppose their doing so.

Shall not Christian women, who owe so much to Christ, be foremost in doing the work allotted to them? What a consummate blunder to live selfishly in this generation! Are we giving the best we have to Christ and to His cause? Christ says, "Whosoever he be of you that forsaketh not all that he hath, he cannot be My disciple." Did Christ only mean that for those who lived hundreds of years ago, or does He mean those words for us to-day? In the presence of a thousand million heathens and Mohammedans needing the Gospel, with multitudes in heathen lands losing faith in their old beliefs and asking for the new, does He not mean those words to-day?

Does He not ask that our time, our money, our influence, our friendships, and our *entire possessions* should be laid at His feet, consecrated to His service, placed absolutely at His disposal? Opportunities such as we have to-day, if neglected, may not come again.

It is said that when the decisive hour in the battle of Waterloo came, the English troops were lying in the trenches, waiting for the onslaught of the enemy. They had been ordered not to fire until the French were close upon them, and while they lay there in silence, Wellington rode up and down the lines saying over and over again, "What will England say to you if you falter now?" One old officer declared that he said it a thousand times, but it is no matter how many times he said it, it was burned into those waiting troops till they felt as if they were lying under the very walls of Parliament, and when the command was given, "Now up, and at them," every man felt that the honour of England was in his hands, and he was invincible.

Do we not hear the voice of a greater Leader saying, "Be thou faithful unto death, and I will give thee a crown of life"? What will the result be if we falter now, if Christians are worldly now, if they are Christians only in name but not in deed, if they only say "Lord, Lord," but do not the things which Christ says? What will Christ think of us if we are not brave and true now?

Let us, at Christ's command, be ready to go forward, for the battle is not ours, but Christ's. Surely we will do well to place ourselves on His side, for we know that in the end His cause shall prevail. We know that all darkness and every evil thing shall be swept away, and that the kingdoms of this world shall become the kingdoms of our Lord and of His Christ. Lord Northbrook recently, at the meeting of the Church Missionary Society, referred to his feelings at hearing Handel's "Hallelujah Chorus" sung. He said it was not so much the music as the words and thoughts that thrilled him. The greatest of all musical creations was inspired by the faith that from sea to sea, and to the ends of the earth, His dominion shall extend, and that from every part of this earth shall yet arise the choral shout, "Hallelujah, for the Lord God Omnipotent reigneth." That is the grander chorus, of which Handel's Hallelujah is but the faint and distant anticipation. It will combine the voices of all loyal, loving saints of all ages, nor is there in all the world, in the obscurest hovel of poverty, one humble soul that prays "Thy Kingdom come," that lays consecrated offerings on the altar of missions, who shall not join that final anthem as one who has helped forward the great consummation.

CHAPTER XXIX.

TOPSY AND THE FAKIR WOMAN.

TOPSY was the name given playfully by a missionary lady in Midnapore, India, to a little girl in her orphanage (whose real name was Sudean), because, like the Topsy in "Uncle Tom's Cabin," she seemed as full of mischief as an egg is full of meat. Her ingenious pranks and practical jokes, perpetrated with a face of intense gravity, caused her school-mates and teachers much annoyance, and drove the missionary lady almost to her wits' end, because she feared that her example might prove contagious among the others. Yet the lady could not dismiss her, for the child, like most others in the school, was a famine orphan, without father or mother or a home of her own, saved from starvation by the kindness of the missionaries.

FAMINE ORPHANS EATING RICE.

One Sabbath, when the missionary was preaching about Christ's death on the cross for us, he noticed Topsy, usually so restless, sitting strangely quiet, and two great tears gathering in her large lustrous eyes, which were fixed upon him. That night Topsy gave her heart to the Saviour who had so loved her as to lay down His life for her. The Good Shepherd had sought and found another of His restless straying lambs. The missionary and his wife rejoiced that night that their labours had not been in vain. From being their greatest cause of anxiety, Topsy became little by little a real comfort and blessing to the orphanage. All her restless energy seemed now turned into channels of service. She asked and obtained permission to go out every day after school hours with an aged Bible-woman, to help her to teach the Bible lessons and Christian hymns to the Zenana women whom she visited.

One day as they were going through the streets, the little girl walking a step or two behind the Bible-woman, as is often the custom in India, Topsy espied a very strange-looking object seated by the roadside on a tiger skin. It was a fakir woman. She was dressed in a very odd yellow dress, her hair all matted as if it had never been combed, her face and arms rubbed with sacred ashes, her neck loaded with numerous necklaces of a kind of sacred nut which fakirs wear, and those who passed by stopped to worship her as a goddess, giving her money, and rubbing the dust from her feet and placing it as something sacred upon their foreheads. Topsy sat down beside her and asked her if she had ever heard about Christ. The fakir woman said she had not, so Topsy began to tell her the story, but before she had finished, the Bible-woman, who had gone on for some distance without missing Topsy, came back to look for her in some alarm, and when she found her, blamed her for stopping behind. Topsy in great distress said to the fakir woman, "I can't stop to tell you the rest now, but if you will come to the house where the missionary lives, this evening, he will be at home then, and he will tell you all about it much better than I can. Be sure to come. I will tell him to expect you." When the Bible-woman and Topsy returned from their daily rounds, Topsy told the missionary about the strange woman who was coming to see him; and though he hardly expected her, sure enough she came, drawn by the magic earnestness of the little girl. Was it not God's answer to the child who prayed and now watched for her appearance?

The missionary received her kindly, and when she was seated told her about Christ and what He had done for us. The fakir woman had never heard this before. He discovered that she was a Brahminee named Chandra Lilavati, and possessed a remarkable education, being able to read in four different languages, viz. Nepalese, Origa, Bengalee, and Hindi, and familiar with many of the sacred books of the Hindus. Her husband, who had been a noted man, a learned Brahmin Pundit, had instructed her and since his death she had wandered during many years all over India on pilgrimages, visiting numerous shrines and temples, and everywhere, on account of her learning and piety, she was worshipped as a goddess. The missionary gave her a gospel in the language most familiar to her, and she went away, only to return again and again, to learn more and more, until she was led to believe in Jesus as the Son of God and to accept Him as her Saviour. On the day when she publicly professed her faith and was baptized, throngs of people came to witness the ceremony, and to see her whom they had formerly worshipped as a goddess renounce all her worldly honours and privileges, and give up her lucrative profession to become a humble follower of Jesus.

After this she begged to be allowed to come daily while the missionary was instructing his class of young Theological Students, and to listen to his words. This was granted to her, and day by day she was found sitting at the missionary's feet with her large-print Bible open on her lap, studying the sacred pages as he tried to expound the precious truths contained in them. It was an inspiration to the missionary to look at her eager, upturned face. Among all his students there was not one who followed him more closely, or who searched the Scriptures more earnestly than she, to see whether these things were so.

When the students were ready to enter upon their work, he said to the woman, "If you would like to become a Bible-woman, I would provide you with a house and give you a salary sufficient to meet your living expenses;" but she answered, "*No, no, I must go back*, and *in every city where I have told the wrong story, I must tell the right one.*" And she who had so long been an object of worship and received every honour and attention, lifted up and placed on her head the heavy basket of Bibles and tracts and religious books with which she had begged the missionary to supply her, and started on foot, though an old woman with white hair, to revisit the cities she had previously visited, and put right what in ignorance she had put wrong.

The missionary heard of her from time to time in Calcutta, Burdwan, Monghir, Lucknow, Cawnpore, Delhi, and other cities in India, the missionaries in these places writing that she had visited them and greatly revived and stimulated their native Christian people by her presence and words, causing great astonishment among the Hindus who had formerly known and worshipped her as a very holy and learned fakir. From time to time she returned to the missionary at Midnapore, bringing back at the end of each journey every penny of the value of the books which she had carried away, and, asking for and obtaining a new supply, she again and again set off on her journeyings, rejoicing in God who had called her to this His work, and who sustained her in it by the conscious presence of His Spirit in her heart.

CHAPTER XXX.

Dasammah, the Little Heroine.

I SHOULD like to tell about a girl who studied in a mission school in India. I will call her Dasammah, though that was not her real name. When she came to the mission school she was about twelve years of age. She was married, but her husband allowed her to attend school. She was a very modest girl, and used to take her seat back in a corner, and draw her cloth closely over her face, so that she should not be much noticed. When questions were asked of her she seemed to be very timid about answering, but the missionary lady noticed that when she was teaching the Bible lesson, this girl seemed always to lean forward and to be drinking in every word. One day when Dasammah went home she told her husband that she did not believe that the idols which they worshipped were true gods, but that she believed that Jesus Christ was the true Saviour. When her husband heard this he was much alarmed, for he feared she would become a Christian. So the next morning he said to her, "Get your things ready quickly; I'm going to take you to live at my mother's house; be ready to leave in an hour."

If you who read these lines were to be told that you were to leave your home and go to a distant village to live, and that you were to be ready to start in an hour, what are the things you would select to take with you? This girl thought of her Bible. But she must not be seen in the street at that time in the morning. So she called a little neighbour girl of lower caste, and said to her, "Run quickly to the missionary's house and get that book we study in the school—the Bible." And the little girl ran to the missionary's house and got a Bible and brought it to Dasammah, and she hid it in her cloth, and that was the only thing she took with her when she went to a distant village to live with her husband's mother. She was the only Christian in that village; there was not a missionary there, or a native pastor, or a native Christian. But day by day she studied her Bible, and day by day the Christ of whom it told became more real and more precious to her.

After a time her husband died suddenly, and then, as is the custom in India, her relatives treated her very cruelly, and charged her with the death of her husband, saying she had used charms or something which had caused his death. The girl said that she had done nothing to cause the death of her husband, but that it was the will of God that he should die at that time. Then they said, "It is because you have given up worshipping our gods, and are worshipping the Christian God. Now you must come back and worship our gods, and promise that you will not become a Christian." The girl said, "Oh, how can I promise that? I *do* believe in Christ. I *am* a Christian." They spoke with her many times on the subject, but she could only give them the one answer—"I *am* a Christian."

One day the men of the house banished all the women to the women's apartments, and taking this little girl out into the yard, drove four stakes into the ground, and tied the girl's hands and feet to these stakes. Then they said to her, "Now we will bring fire and burn your feet, unless you promise that you'll not become a Christian." And the girl answered, "I *do* believe in Christ. I am a Christian." They put the fire to her feet and let it burn them, and the pain was very great. Then they said to her, "Now will you promise that you'll not become a Christian?" The girl answered, "Oh, I cannot promise, I am, *I am a Christian.*" Surely He who walked with the three children of Israel in the burning, fiery furnace, was with this poor girl, and strengthened her in the hour of her great trial. After a time, the pain was so great she could not bear it, and she fainted away. When the men saw that, they were afraid she would die, and that the English Government might call them to account for their conduct. So they untied her hands and feet, and then carried her away into a dark room, and left her there. In the middle of the night consciousness returned to her, and she got up and felt for the door, and found it was open. She went out and made straight for the missionary's house. It took her that night, and the next day, and late into the next night, to reach it. She walked part of the way, as well as she could, on her poor sore feet, and when she could not travel thus any further, she got down and crawled on her hands and knees. When she came to the missionary's house, she knocked. The missionary lady came to the door and looked at the girl, but did not recognize her, she was so covered with dust and looked so wretched. She said to the girl, "Who are you?" The girl told her. Then she asked, "Why did you come?" The girl said, "*I believe on the Lord Jesus Christ, and I want to be baptized.*"

The missionary lady took her in, and when she saw what a condition her feet were in, she was very sorry for her. She dressed her feet, and all the time she was doing this the girl never uttered a single murmur or complaint, but only said, "Oh, how good you are! how you must love Jesus Christ, to be so kind to a poor girl like me!"

After a time her feet healed, and she said to the missionary lady, "You have a Bible-woman who visits in the homes and teaches the women; I should so like to help her to tell the women about Christ. I could live on very little, all I should want would be rice and salt; two shillings a month would be quite sufficient to buy my food. If you could find some one who would pay that for me, I would spend my whole time teaching the women in the homes." The missionary lady furnished her with the needed means, and she is now a Bible-woman, and very happy in her work. This girl had only known about Christ a short time, but He was very precious to her, and she desired to tell others about Him.

I wonder if you who read these lines love Christ as much, and if you are letting your light shine as brightly. If Christ were to stand before you in bodily form, and say to you as He said to His disciples, "*As My Father hath sent Me, even so send I you,*" how would you feel in His presence? Would you be able to look into His dear face and say, "*Lord Jesus, I do desire to be in the world as Thou wast in the world. Make me more and more to be like Thee.*"

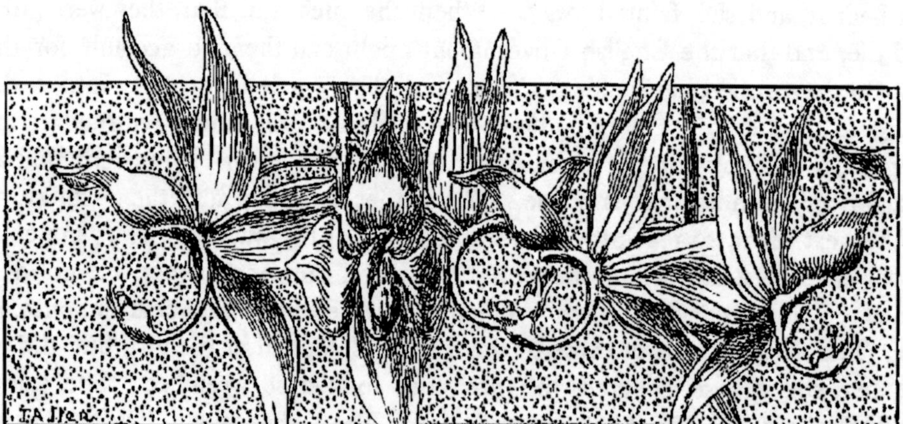

OTLEY HALL, JAFFNA COLLEGE.

CHAPTER XXXI.

The Jaffna College.

THE Jaffna College, situated at Batticotta in North Ceylon, is, as far as we know, the first attempt of a Christian community in a heathen land to establish a college of their own.

It originated in a *spontaneous effort, made by the native Christians of Jaffna* in 1867, to establish a Christian College, which should give a superior education both in the English and vernacular languages. A meeting of educated Tamils was called, and was largely attended. At this meeting a scheme was adopted, and a committee appointed to collect funds and take initiatory steps toward establishing a Christian College. Principally through the efforts of this native committee, £1700 *were raised in Ceylon*—a large sum, when it is remembered that in Jaffna the wage of a labouring man is only sixpence a day. The people of America, hearing of this effort on the part of the native Christians, and believing those most worthy of help who try to help themselves, contributed £6000, and the

American Board of Missions gave, for the use of the College, land and buildings worth £5000.

Early in 1872 the College was started under the general management and control of a Board of Directors. *This Board of Directors is at present composed of the senior missionaries of the three Missions working in Jaffna, namely, the Church of England Mission, the Wesleyan Mission, and the American Mission ; along with the Government Agent of the Northern Province, and representative native Christian gentlemen of the community.*

The Jaffna College, it will be noted, is *not a denominational institution.* It is not controlled by any one missionary body, though it has the sympathy and direction of the three missionary societies which are at work in Jaffna. *It is a thoroughly Christian institution* The Rev. E. P. Hastings, M.A., D.D., who had been for twenty-five years a missionary of the American Mission in Jaffna, was invited to preside over the institution as its first Principal, and he continued to fill the office with great acceptance for seventeen years. His unwearied devotion for over forty years to the people of Jaffna enabled him to win the confidence and affection of the whole community. Having resigned his position in June, 1889, the Rev. S. W. Howland, M.A., for sixteen years a missionary of the American Mission in Jaffna, was chosen as his successor.

Besides the Principal, there are in the College two foreign professors who hold the degree of B.A., and five able native professors, *all of whom are Christians. There has never been a heathen teacher employed in the College, and it is hoped there never will be*, for it is believed that one heathen teacher in an institution like this could undo the work of many Christian teachers. It is desired that this be first of all a Christian College, with the current all one way.

REV E. P. HASTINGS, D.D.,
For nineteen years Principal of Jaffna College.

A PROFESSOR AND STUDENTS IN JAFFNA COLLEGE.

There are at present 167 students, with seven teachers, in the High School, a preparatory school for the College, and about 100 students in the College itself. It is a rule of the College that all the students reside on the premises. *They are thus separated from heathen influence, and are under the strongest Christian influence continuously, refraining from all heathen practices, even from wearing the idolatrous marks on their foreheads.* Yet so great is the desire for education in the community, and so highly is the education prized which is given, that many *Hindu young men of high-caste are willing to enter this Christian College as boarders*, paying the full cost of board, also £1 as entrance fee, and £3 for tuition annually. These high-caste Hindu young men are accustomed to eat, sleep, and live with the Christian students, to be present at morning and evening prayers, to study the Bible daily, to attend the weekly prayer-meetings, also Sabbath-school, church service, and Bible-class on Sabbath.

So greatly has God blessed the College that, of the 326 who have entered its doors, 142 *have gone out into the world as professed Christians and communicants; others have professed Christ after leaving the College, and the majority of the nearly* 100 *students at present in the College are Christians. Many of the graduates of the institution have become pastors, catechists, and teachers, not only in missions in Ceylon, but also in India.*

It has been said, "*Whatever you would put into the life of a nation, put into its schools.*" *The teachings of Christ are given the first place in the College,* and He is held up as the one perfect model for imitation. His words, "I came not to be ministered unto, but to minister," and "My meat is to do the will of Him that sent Me," are sounded as the key-note for every one who would make his life harmonize with the Divine ideal.

There is in the College an active Young Men's Christian Association. The members of this association not only labour for the conversion of the Hindu students in the College, but also do much valuable work outside. On Sabbath afternoons they regularly go out and conduct six Sabbath schools in the neighbouring villages. These Sabbath schools are attended by nearly 400 children. Not content with this, they have originated and for the past three or four years supported a school in an island lying near Jaffna, called Ninathevu. They have built a school-bungalow, and have paid for several years the whole salary of the teacher. It may be interesting to know how the young men are able to raise the money for his support. There is a piece of land belonging to the college grounds which the members of the Y.M.C.A. cultivate as a garden, selling the produce for the benefit of the school; and while some of their companions are playing cricket or other games in the recreation hours, they are hard at work, hoeing, watering, walking the well-sweep, &c., &c.

A number of young men, graduates of the College, have studied theology and entered upon evangelistic work. Were they to engage in secular employment under the Government, they might expect to receive a salary of from £5 to £10 a month, with a prospect of promotion, but they have voluntarily chosen the work of preachers of the Gospel, with a salary of £1 10*s.* to begin with, and a prospect of not more than £3 or £4, as few pastors in Jaffna receive more than £4 a month as salary. We feel that they have made this choice out of love to Christ, and a desire to serve Him. They show a similar spirit to that shown by a Burmese boatman who, when converted, was earning £6 a month. Perceiving that he was a ready speaker and clever withal, the missionary said to him one day: "Can you give up your business and preach to your countrymen? I may be able to give you half-a-pound a month for this. Can you do it?" The man thought a moment, then replied with a beaming face and tears in his eyes: "No, I can't do it for the half-pound a month, but I can do it for the love of the Lord Jesus Christ." We believe it is the same spirit which is animating many of the Jaffna College graduates.

About five years ago there came a request from the missionary at Indore, Scindia,

India, for a graduate of the College to come as a teacher of English in the Mission High School there. Mr. Chanmukam, a graduate who had been converted during his College course, consented to go. In the meantime there came a second letter from the missionary, saying that as they were in the territory of a native prince who was unfavourable to the introduction of Christianity, they met with much opposition in their mission work: that they were not allowed to buy or rent a house in the city, but had to live and teach in buildings outside of the city; that when they held preaching services, the native police often broke up the meetings, dispersing the people, and even taking the native helpers to prison. Mr. Chanmukam was called, and the letter was read to him. While he listened, tears began slowly to gather in his eyes. At its close he looked up with a radiant and determined face and said: "If that missionary can leave his home and come all the way to India and endure all that for the sake of Christ, I think I ought to go and help him." And he went with a true missionary spirit to a country 1600 miles distant from Jaffna, among a people who speak another language, and where the climate, food, dress, religion, all are different.

The missionary wrote as follows of him and of another Jaffna College graduate who has more recently gone to the same place:—

PORTRAIT OF MR. CHANMUKAM.

Indore, Central India, *October* 1, 1886.

In reply to your letter, I most gladly bear testimony in regard to Mr. Chanmukam and Mr. Charles, two Jaffna graduates at Indore, the former of whom I have had ample opportunity of testing, as he has been with me now for about two years.

Mr. Chanmukam is very well up in English, Mathematics, History, Geography, Grammar, &c., as is seen from the fact that he so easily at the last Entrance Examination of the Calcutta University stood first in English and Mathematics, and fourth in all the subjects. His knowledge of the first two is superior to that of many of the B.A.'s that we have about us here. As a teacher, he has been most successful both in winning the confidence of the boys and in imparting knowledge, and is to-day the favourite teacher in the school, as well as the best. So much confidence have I in him, that as soon as his place here can be filled, I intend to send him to Ujjain to start and take charge of a new High-School which I hope soon to start there. What especially has pleased me has been his modest, earnest consistent Christian life—an example that alone has done much to help us here. His duties do not allow him much time for direct Christian work, yet where he gets opportunity he does not fail to use it. My earnest wish is for more such men, and my warmest thanks are due to the Institution which trained him, to you for sending him, and to the Grace of God above all, which has in him so manifestly shown to the heathen its power.

Though of Mr. Charles I cannot speak so fully, as he has been a shorter time with us, yet we all like very much his earnest, faithful efforts, which as time goes on will be more appreciated I doubt not.

With thanks for your kind interest in our work, I remain, yours sincerely.

J. WILKIE, *Canadian Mission.*

More than five years ago a call came from a missionary at Ahmednagar, in the Deccan, India, for a teacher in the mission college there. Mr. Lee, a graduate of the Jaffna College, a native Christian of the third generation, accepted the call. The missionary wrote of him :—

Ahmednagar, Deccan, India, *June* 28, 1886.

Two years ago you sent a young man to help us here—Mr. G. C. Lee. We are *more* than satisfied with him as a scholar, teacher, and above all as a *Christian.* I congratulate you on turning out such a man. He is more than I hoped for, and has become by far the best man I have or have had. Had I some more like him, with a good knowledge of Marathi, I could have the best school in India. As it is, his work could not be better done by any one, and besides, he is always at my elbow to do anything and everything.

With best wishes, yours very truly,

JAMES SMITH, *American Missionary,*
Principal, Ahmednagar College.

After this young man had been in Ahmednagar for some time on a salary of £4 a month, he received an offer of £10 a month if he would go elsewhere, but he said, "No ; I think I can do more good here," and he stayed. He teaches large classes of high-caste Hindu young men, and he has so won their friendship and esteem that students of his classes often go to his room in the evening for conversation on religious subjects, and for Bible-reading and prayer. His brother, also a graduate of the Jaffna College, is likewise now employed in the same Institution.

Numbers of Jaffna young men are employed in similar capacities and with much

MR. G. C. LEE (IN THE CENTRE) AND A FEW OF HIS STUDENTS.

acceptance in Bombay, Madras, Ujjain, Coimbatoon, Roha, Madura Passumallui, and other parts of India, as well as in Rangoon and Singapore. *God has given to many of the graduates a missionary spirit, and a willingness to leave home and go to all parts of India on small salaries, to engage in the work of teaching in mission schools. In this fact seems to lie an indication of Providence as to the work before the College in the future, to which we should take heed, and in which we should rejoice.*

It is now proposed to make the Jaffna College a First-Grade College; to extend its course of study; to add to its staff of foreign and native professors; enlarging and improving its building accommodation, reducing the general expenses, and providing permanent scholarships in aid of necessitous students. At the present time the Jaffna College enables its students to pass the Cambridge Junior and Senior Local Examinations, and gives a select course of study beyond that. But if larger and larger numbers of the graduates of the Jaffna College are to find places as teachers in Mission Schools in India, this College must be affiliated with a University, for the Educational Department of the Madras Presidency has lately passed a resolution that only those who have matriculated or who hold degrees will be eligible to receive salary grants from Government. As it is by these grants that Indian Mission Colleges are largely supported, Indian missionaries will be unable to employ Jaffna graduates hereafter, to any large extent, unless they comply with this Government requirement. The Mission Colleges in India are doing a great work in giving a Christian education to the youths of India, and stemming the tide of infidelity which is coming in like a flood, owing to the fact that only a secular education is given in Government Colleges.

Major-General F. T. Haig, R.E., writes as follows respecting Government education in India :—

"There is a great thirst for education throughout India. Education is spreading like wildfire. Hindoos are already beginning to tax themselves for education, and that will be the most popular tax in the country. But observe what is being done. The Government are in earnest in this matter. They are going in for the education of these 250 millions. But it will be a *godless* education. There is not even the Bible in the Indian school; it is utterly put aside, and the education given is absolutely secular. What is to be the result? *What will be the vast social and political movement that will take place among* 250 *millions of people, whose faith in their own ancestral religion has been destroyed by their education, and to whom we have given nothing else?* A statesman, however worldly, might be appalled at the prospect of having to deal with such a people, and yet that is what we have got before us, unless the Christian Church will do its duty, and impart to the people that religious instruction which cannot be given in the Government schools.

"We have in India 250 millions of people, 200 millions of whom are our fellow-subjects; for they are really and truly subjects of the Queen. The remaining 50 millions are the subjects of the feudatory States, in each of which we have a resident without whose permission nothing can be done. *For all these millions, who are practically our fellow-subjects, we are doubly responsible before God.* We have subdued the country in the most perfect manner, and we are responsible before God for the welfare of its people. We cannot put this thought aside. We may ignore the remainder of the heathen world if we will, but these 250 millions of India we cannot set aside. We must feel that we are responsible before God for them and for their salvation. What is the spiritual provision that we as a Christian people are now making for the people of India? Let us just for one moment remember the provision that we make for our own spiritual needs at home:—

"In England we have 20,000 clergymen of the Church of England and at least as many more ministers of the different Nonconformist denominations. Then for each one of these clergymen and ministers you must allow several additional classes of Christian workers, like city missionaries, Sunday-school teachers, visitors, Bible-women, and every conceivable form of paid and unpaid Christian labourers. Taking simply the clergymen and ministers who are specially ordained for this work, we have at least 40,000 in this little island ministering to the religious wants of 26 millions of people, *or one to every* 650 *people.*

"Now, let us look to British India. What have we got there? Six hundred and forty ministers, *or one to every* 450,000 *people.* Please note these facts. The facts with regard to the heathen world at large are very few and simple, but of enormous power. We send to India, where we have been these two hundred years, only 640 ministers! Is there not something monstrously wrong there?"

We would like to insert also an extract from a non-Christian Hindu paper, the *Indu Prakash* of Bombay:—

"Education provided by the State simply destroys Hinduism; it gives nothing in its place. It is founded on the benevolent principle of non-interference with religion, but in practice it is the negation of God in life. Education must destroy idolatry, and the State education of India, benevolent in its idea, practically teaches atheism. It leaves its victims faithless. Our young men are, many of them, forced by it into the unhappy position of the sceptics and infidels of Europe. As soon as this is generally perceived and felt, the cry will go up to England, 'Father, Father, give us faith!' Knowledge alone does not suffice men, nor material prosperity, nor good government; the things of this life are fleeting, the life to come is eternal; and men and nations can only be happy in recognizing and acting righteously on this Divine fact. Without faith, life is without an aim, death without hope, and there can be neither individual happiness nor national greatness. If England will not hear our cry, and indeed anticipate it, then will the shriek go up to our Father in heaven, 'Father, Father, give us faith.'"

Is not this appeal most touching, considering the source from whence it comes? Will not Christians respond to it, and do *more* to support the Christian Colleges of India and Ceylon, and Christian work in every department?

A missionary in Lucknow, India, writes:—

"We in India are in the midst of a great educational movement. The intellect of these people is awaking from the sleep of twenty centuries, and everywhere the youth

TRICHINOPOLY ROCK AND TEMPLE.

may be seen thronging toward the schoolroom. We have boldly entered the country and challenged Buddhism, Mahommedanism, and Hinduism to combat, and now we have no alternative short of retreat left us save that of manfully trying to meet the momentous responsibilities which the intellectual awakening has imposed upon us. We cannot confine our work to preaching alone. As well try to persuade the churches at home to abolish their colleges and seminaries. We have no choice. To shirk our responsibility would be to postpone the final triumph of Christianity for generations to come, and consign the intellect of the country to a depraved infidelity compounded of the superstition of the Hindu, the bigotry of the Mahommedan, the lethargy of the Buddhist, and the Sadducean heartlessness of the European rationalist. Christianity must at once assume her full responsibility in trying to guide this educational movement, so as to make it a blessing instead of a curse to India."

The missionaries in India are thus striving in a devoted spirit, and with a large measure of success, to impart a sound religious and secular education to the vast number of youths who throng into their institutions. But it is widely felt that the *Indian Mission Colleges labour as yet under one great difficulty, viz. the lack of a sufficient number of able Christian teachers of good caste.*

While recently in India we visited the following colleges:—Wesleyan College, Negapatam; S. P. G. College, Tanjore: S. P. G. College, Trichinopoly; Free Church College, Madras; Free Church College, Bombay; Free Church College, Poona; London Mission College, Calcutta; American Methodist Mission College, Lucknow. We found in these great institutions, in the preparatory and collegiate departments, altogether 5030 students; of these, 374 were Christians. We found 163 native teachers, fifty-one of whom were Christians and 112 of whom were non-Christians. These facts speak for themselves as to the need of additional Christian teachers for the mission colleges of India. The Hindu and Mahommedan teachers, as a rule, outnumber the native Christian teachers. It is not unusual to find, in Indian Mission Colleges and High Schools, Brahmin teachers, with heathen marks on their foreheads, sitting before their students in the class rooms teaching B.A and F.A. subjects, while the native Christian teachers take lower subjects, and sometimes a Pariah or Shanar native pastor teaches the Bible lesson. This, as can be easily seen, tends to make an unfavourable impression on the minds of the students in regard to the value and importance of Christianity. It may be partly as a result of this that many Indian Mission Colleges have to report so comparatively small a number of conversions among their students. Mission Colleges will never be such powerful evangelizing agencies as they ought to be until this state of things is rectified. *The missionaries themselves deplore it, and would most gladly fill the places of these heathen teachers with Christian men of influence and thorough education, if enough of such could be obtained.* The Principal of the Lucknow American Mission College writes in a recent annual report, speaking of that large mission: "The demand in all parts of the field is rapidly increasing: we could employ two hundred Christian teachers at once were they available; as it is we are obliged to employ Hindu and Mahommedan teachers."

It is to be borne in mind that the Christian community in India is comparatively small as yet (one in 1000 of the population), and is composed mostly of converts from the low caste or outcast classes, and not from those who are Hindus proper. The low castes, having been ground down by poverty and oppression for centuries, are mentally inferior to the high castes, and many would not be intellectually able to take a full B.A. course in English. Besides, the low caste as a rule are poor, and therefore most of them have not the means to give their sons an extended education.

Now, turning and viewing the facts in Jaffna, we find an almost opposite state of things. The English and American missions, by God's providence and blessing, have been able largely to evangelize the upper castes. There are in the churches of the three missions in Jaffna over 2500 communicants, or nearly one in 100 of the population, mostly of high caste, and there are in the Christian day-schools of these missions 15,000 children, also mostly of high caste. Educated Jaffna Christians are, as a rule, able and reliable men. A former Governor of Madras, Sir Charles Trevelyan, said that he found no young men so useful to him in administration of affairs as those trained in the College (Seminary) at Jaffna. *We believe that this is Jaffna's great opportunity to help India, and that with God's blessing Jaffna may prove to be a key to India in reaching its upper castes.* India is very accessible from Ceylon, and native boats can cross to India in a night.

Were the Jaffna College well equipped and affiliated with a University, Christian graduates could be sent as helpers to many missions in India. Who can tell how great a service this would be rendering to missions, and to the cause of Christ in India? Just as formerly missionaries from the little island of Iona went over Scotland, and Scotland is now a Christian land, so from the island of Ceylon shall go, we trust, in the future, many native Christian workers to India, and, by God's blessing, help to make that great land one day a Christian land. With 15,000 children, mostly of high caste, in the Christian day-schools of the missions, a large proportion of whom are bright, promising lads, eager for an education and able and willing to pay for it in whole or in part, should not the College endeavour to train as many as possible for Christian work in Ceylon and India?

Almost the whole education of the peninsula is in the hands of the missionaries, and the parents, as a rule, do not object to their children learning the Bible lessons and Christian songs, nor to their attending the Sabbath-school. Young men and women from heathen families of good caste, on becoming Christians and joining the Church, seldom meet now with any great persecution from their relatives, but are generally allowed to live as Christians in their homes, eating with the other members of the family. Child marriage is not practised as in India, and widow re-marriage is becoming more common. The Zenana system of India does not prevail, though girls and young women of good families are kept in some seclusion. Caste prejudices are not so strong as in India. The people are not so priest-ridden, and many are losing faith in idolatry. Almost every house is open to visits of the missionaries and native helpers, and Christianity, instead of being bitterly opposed and looked down upon, is generally respected in the community. These and other advantageous circumstances fit Jaffna to be *a nursery for Christian workers.* In this favourable atmosphere they may develop strong, vigorous, well-balanced Christian characters.

Missionaries alone cannot accomplish the vast work of reaching and evangelizing the 250 millions of India. The missionary force on the ground is small (one ordained missionary to 450,000 people). It is by natives that the bulk of the work must be done. Hence the urgent necessity to train and send forth a large and well-qualified staff of native agents. A native can get nearer to the people than a foreigner, can understand better their difficulties, feels more free with the language, and is not affected by the tropical sun as a foreigner is apt to be. Viewing the matter also from a financial standpoint, we find that the cost of educating and maintaining native workers is trifling compared with the cost of educating, sending out, and maintaining foreigners.

The cost of educating a student in the Jaffna College, including food, clothing, books, incidentals, and tuition, does not exceed £10 a year. It need scarcely be said that care is taken not to allow the students to learn extravagant habits. They wear the native dress, eat the native food of the country, and live in the simplest native style *Hence the graduates are willing to become pastors, catechists, and evangelists on small salaries*, supplied entirely by native churches. Of the twenty-two native churches in Jaffna, the majority are self-supporting.

In a recent conversation with a missionary from India, who had been for many years connected with a missionary college in one of the Presidency towns, he said, "Our great difficulty is that, though we have native Christian young men graduating from our college every year, we cannot secure them, as a rule, for mission helpers. The reason is that the Government offers twice or thrice as much salary as our mission is able to give, and the temptation proves too much for them, so they enter Government service."

But the glory of the Jaffna College is that many of its graduates do not want to

MR. EDWIN R. FITCH (A GRADUATE OF THE JAFFNA COLLEGE), HEAD MASTER IN THE ENGLISH MIDDLE SCHOOL OF THE CANADIAN MISSION IN UJJAIN, AND SOME OF HIS ASSISTANTS AND PUPILS.

engage in Government service, but seek mission work, even though the pay may be only one-half or one-third of what they could get in secular employments. They have found something better worth living for than making money. It has been said, "There has never been such giving toward religious objects as has been shown by Hindus in their worship, and if they have done this for false gods, what may we not expect of them when they know the true God?" May we not hope that the native Christians may more and more in the future possess the Spirit of Him who said, "I have meat to eat that ye know not of," and "My meat is to do the will of Him that sent Me."

It was most touching to note in the *Church Missionary Intelligencer* for September, 1887, that two young men, natives of Syria, graduating from the American Mission College at Beirut, on hearing of the martyrdoms taking place in Uganda, offered themselves to the Church Missionary Society for mission work in Africa. They knew the difficulties and dangers of the work, the climate, the degradation of the people, but they said, "We have taken all this into account, and we wish to go to Africa and to live and die if need be for that people." They made no stipulations as to salary or kind of work. They were mindful of their Master's last words, "Ye shall be witnesses of Me . . . unto the uttermost part of the earth." Obedience is simply a question of supreme love to Christ.

When Garibaldi had been defeated at Rome, he issued his immortal appeal: "Soldiers, I have nothing to offer you but cold, and hunger, and rags, and hardships; let him who loves his country follow me:" and thousands of youths of Italy sprang to their feet. If the young men and young women in Christian lands love their own ease and comfort too much to follow Jesus to the mission-field, surely the time is coming when the very stones will cry out, and from among the converted heathen those shall arise who will improve the great opportunity, which others have despised, of evangelizing the whole world.

Jaffna College graduates could readily engage in evangelistic work not only in Ceylon but all over South India, as the *Tamil language*, which is the vernacular in Jaffna, is the language of sixteen millions of people in Southern India.

"In towns and villages much work can be done by those whose scholastic attainments are not high—earnest, humble workers, labouring among their own relatives. But besides these, we must have for the larger places well-educated helpers, able to answer the numerous and often difficult objections which their opponents bring forward. But, apart from the growing demand for first-class preachers, the country urgently requires a class of educated native Christians, capable in different spheres of usefulness of influencing other educated natives all around them. And it must not be forgotten that our plans, having for their object the perfect independence of the native churches, are sure to prove abortive if native Christians are not prepared by superior education for the responsible and remunerative posts which have hitherto been monopolized by Hindus, Mussulmans, Buddhists, and Eurasians."

There are in Jaffna over 2500 native Christian communicants. "A well-equipped college would be the greatest boon to this raipdly-increasing native Christian community, insuring to the sons of native converts educational facilities which otherwise they could not enjoy, and thus giving them a preparation which would fit them for lives of the highest Christian usefulness. We want not only a warm-hearted but a strong, intelligent, clear-headed native Church. We would not be content to have our converts and their children remain on the same low level of intelligence where the Gospel found them. We wish for them growth, advancement, success; and one of the wisest methods of insuring these is to build up this college, the uplifting influence of which will be felt for generations to come."

REQUIREMENTS.

		Fund.	Yearly Income.
Endowment for the Salary of Principal		£5,000	£250
Endowment for the Salary of one Married Foreign Professor		5,000	250
Endowment for One-Third Salary of Married Foreign Medical Professor		2,000	100
Endowment for the Salary of Native Medical Professor...		1,100	55
Endowment for the Salaries of three Native Professors...		4,500	225
Permanent Scholarships of £100 each for 60 Students (Ten of these Permanent Scholarships are for Medical Students.)		6,000	300
General Endowment		4,500	225
House and Furniture for Married Foreign Professor	£600		
Building Sites and Houses for Three Native Professors	300		
Improvement of College—Dining Hall	100		
Laboratory and Physical Science Hall with additional Apparatus	300		
New Dormitories	200		
Library Building and Library	200		
General Improvements on existing Buildings ...	200		
		1,900	
Total sum required		...£30.000	

The foregoing Estimates of Requirements received the sanction of the Board of Directors of the Jaffna College.

NAMES OF DIRECTORS.

Foreign Residents.

W. C. Twynam, Esq., C.M.G. Government Agent, Northern Province.

Rev. E. P. Hastings, D.D , M.A., American Missionary, Principal Jaffna College.

Rev. W. W. Howland, M.A., American Missionary.

Rev. R. C. Hastings, M.A., American Missionary.

Rev. E. M. Griffith, M.A., Church Missionary.

Rev. W. R. Winston, Wesleyan Missionary, Chairman Northern Ceylon District.

Native Residents.

C. W. CATHIRAVALU PILLAI, Esq., Magistrate.
R. BRECKENBRIDGE, Esq., Sub-Inspector of Schools.
Rev. E. CHAMPION, Native Pastor, Church Mission.
Rev. B. H. RICE, Native Pastor, American Mission.
J. R. ARNOLD, Esq., Joint Editor, *Morning Star.*
Rev. T. P. HUNT, Native Pastor American Mission.
T. C. CHANGARA PILLAI, Esq., Proctor, Supreme Court.
T. M. TAMBU, Esq., Proctor, Supreme Court.
L. S. STRONG, Esq., Medical Practitioner.
WM. PAUL, Esq., Dispenser, Friend-in-Need Hospital.
J. P. COOKE, Esq., Head Master, Batticotta High School.

We hope that friends of education and of Christianity will aid this enterprise. £30,000 may seem to be a large sum, but is it large considering what is proposed to be accomplished by it, viz. the extending and permanently endowing of a Christian College, and a General Medical Mission? A lady in Glasgow gave recently £12,500 to endow one additional chair in the Glasgow University, where already they have 50 professors and teachers.

It is proposed to have 180 students in the College. Of these, 120 will be required to pay the whole cost of their education, viz. £10 a year, and the remaining 60, or one-third of the whole number, we wish to be able to aid by scholarships to the extent of one-half of their expenses, or £5 a year.

There are in our Missions pastors and catechists of good ability receiving only £2 or £3 per month, who might have been receiving, had they sought Government employment, £8 or £10 a month, and yet, from love to Christ and to His cause, they have chosen Christian work. Scholarships could sometimes be used in aiding the sons of these Christian workers, for they must find it very difficult to pay the whole sum required to give their sons a college education; and we have reason to hope that such boys, if taken into the College, would become useful Christian workers in their turn, having been from earliest childhood brought up in the atmosphere of a Christian home.

Over 50 Bible-women are employed under the three missions in Jaffna. They receive from 8*s.* to 16*s.* a month as salary. A considerable number of these are widows who support themselves and their little ones on this small sum. To aid sons of these Bible-women by scholarships would be a truly Christian deed. When a native Christian mother, a widow, has dedicated her most precious treasure, her eldest son, to mission work, surely it should be a joy for fathers and mothers in a Christian country to help such a one pecuniarily in the education of that son, and so share in the blessing which is sure to follow.

£100 will found a permanent scholarship. It might bear the name of the founder, or, if given by a congregation, Sunday-school, or Bible-class, the name of the pastor, school superintendent, or teacher. When not convenient to pay the whole sum at once, it might be paid in instalments of £20 a year for five years. Many who cannot themselves afford such sums, yet out of love for the cause might be able to interest a circle of ten friends who would each undertake to give £2 a year for five years; thus a whole scholarship would be secured. An annual subscription of £5 would be equal to a temporary scholarship. Students will write yearly letters to their patrons, giving accounts of their studies and progress.

Only Christian young men will be aided by scholarships or annual subscriptions. Each young man so aided will sign an undertaking that he will engage in mission work under some Mission in Ceylon or India for a period of years after his graduation; or that, if he is in any way prevented from doing this, he will refund to the College all the money which he has received from the scholarship. Thus the scholarships will aid in training up native Christians pledged to mission work.

A Scotch laird once said to his son, "Aye be stickin' in a tree, Jamie; it'll be growin' when ye're sleepin'." We think that to be endowing a scholarship in a Christian college in a heathen land is to be sticking in a tree which will be growing while we are sleeping in the dust, or rather when we have left this earth and are rejoicing in the presence of our Saviour.

A missionary of long experience in India, when at home on furlough, wrote as follows:—

"The people in heathen lands can worship in private houses, or under trees, or in the open street with little aid from outside, but they imperatively need help in the matter of Christian education. Without it the churches cannot flourish, their children will grow up in ignorance; there is no assurance that the Christian life which has been begun in them will retain its hold upon the next generation. The honest, earnest cry for a training which shall produce a native evangelical agency, both as preachers and teachers, is coming up from all quarters. In some cases it is a piercing cry! It is a call not for a luxury but for a necessity. It ought to be heard and heeded. Missionaries who are temporarily at home open the papers and find every week or two, perhaps oftener, the record of a gift of ten or twenty thousand pounds sterling to this or that college or other institution of learning. Perhaps it may be for a professorship, in addition to the twenty, or thirty, or forty others now secured. Perhaps it may be for an art gallery or a gymnasium, or some other desirable thing in connection with the institution. They are not narrow-minded men and women who do not appreciate the importance of having everything that may tend to the development of the generations to come. But they cannot help saying within themselves, "That gift of £20,000; it will add something to the value of a prosperous college, but it would found for all time a whole institution in our field. It would at once open the way for a Christian education to scores and scores of young men, who, without it, will have no opportunity to fit themselves as preachers or teachers. If missionaries do not ask that some of the luxuries which are provided for institutions of learning in this country be curtailed a little, is it not right that they should ask for some of the crumbs that fall from the table, so that the people for whom they labour may not be left to starve?"

We have been sometimes asked how we were led first of all to undertake the work of securing the needed funds for this institution. In North Ceylon there were ten missionary families among a population of 316,000 people. Each family had charge of a district. We were the only missionaries in a district of 20,000 people. There were in our district twenty-six day-schools, with about 2000 children in them. Of these, several were English schools. Two of these, with a total attendance of about 200 students, were situated near the mission house, and the majority of the students attended our station Sabbath-school. The upper classes from both schools also came to our house daily for a Bible lesson in English, and for help in their secular studies. Having them thus with us daily, both during the week and in our Sunday-school classes, we became deeply interested in them, and regarded them as younger brothers. Most of them came from heathen homes, and wore the marks of the god Siva on their foreheads, yet we noticed, as we went on teaching them the truth, that without our asking them to do so, one after another began of their own accord to leave off the heathen marks. Many of them began to attend the church services, several joined the inquirers' class, and some from time to time professed faith in Christ, and were received into the Church. We knew that many more were, in their hearts, really convinced of the truth of the Gospel, and were just at the turning-point of their lives.

Many of these boys, on leaving the English day-schools, were desirous of a higher education. What would they do? Some would go to the Jaffna College and ask to be received, but the college has at present limited accommodation, and perhaps they could not pay the required fees. Perhaps of twenty boys leaving the English day-schools in our district each year, two or three would be received into the college. What would the others do? They were *determined* to have a higher education. They would go to India, to study in heathen or non-Christian schools, where they could live in the houses of their heathen relations, and be aided in their expenses by

IMAGE OF ONE OF THE FIVE "PANDIANS" IN TREVANDRUM FORT.

THE CRUEL GODDESS KALI.

heathen relatives. We have known fourteen of our dear boys, whom we had taught for years, and had learned to love, go over to India in one night, most of them to study in that sink of iniquity and moral leprosy—Kompa-kornum.

We knew that these boys would board in heathen families, would be compelled the first night, before they ate their food, to put on the heathen ashes, and to wear them always; that they would not be allowed to attend any Christian services, but would be obliged to go to temples, perform heathen ceremonies, study the heathen books; that they would hear Christ constantly reviled, and the Christian religion mocked and scorned, and that being under these influences for a period of years, they would come back to us bitter heathens, or agnostics, or infidels, to be our worst opposers, and morally unfit to become the husbands of the pure young girls who were being trained in mission day and boarding schools, to whom in many instances they were engaged.

When we were in India in 1882, and again in 1885, we took occasion to visit the cities of Negapatam, Tanjore, Trichinopoly, Madura, and Madras, and to see the Jaffna young men who were studying in the heathen or Government schools in those cities. It pained our hearts to find them living among heathen surroundings, and to see how worldly and irreligious they

A GROUP OF CHRISTIAN SINGERS.

(PONNIAH WITH THE VIOLIN.)

had grown, and how far they had retrograded since they had left us in Jaffna. We knew that had these young men been studying instead in the Jaffna College, under the strong Christian influence there, they would in all probability, with God's blessing, have given their hearts to Christ, and been preparing for lives of Christian usefulness in Ceylon or in India.

As we went on teaching large classes of boys from year to year, on week-days and Sabbaths, loving them, labouring and praying for their conversion, seeing them almost persuaded to be Christians, and then at the critical moment finding large numbers of the brightest and most promising leave us year by year for these heathen schools in India, it seemed as though we could not bear it. We made a census of the peninsula of Jaffna, and found that about 200 Jaffna young men were then studying in schools outside of Jaffna. When we pictured to ourselves the almost overpoweringly evil influences with which we had seen them surrounded in India, and the effect these must have on their characters; and when we reflected that were the Jaffna College enlarged and its course of instruction extended, many of these students might have been kept in Jaffna instead of being allowed to go to India away from parental restraint and from all Christian influence; and as we heard at the Union Missionary Prayer Meetings the missionaries of all the three societies in Jaffna again and again deplore the existing state of things; we felt that something ought to be done, that it was not enough merely to deplore the evil thing, that we ought to try to remedy it. The thought also of the good these young men of high caste might do, if brought to Christ, in replacing heathen teachers in mission schools in India, was constantly present to our minds.

A circumstance which took place at that time helped to lead us to a decision. We were told, one afternoon, that a boy named Ponniah was going to be sent by his parents to India the next day. We were specially attached to this bright young Christian boy, the son of Christian parents. He was always ready to do Christian work; he was a sweet singer, and had constantly assisted us by singing at our open air and village meetings. We went at once to the house. We spoke as earnestly as we could with the parents, begging them not to send their son to India. They said, "What can we do? We have, as you know, a large family of little children, and Ponniah must be educated, that he may be able to help his younger brothers and sisters. We are unable to educate him in Jaffna College. We have asked the

A PROFESSOR AND STUDENTS IN THE JAFFNA COLLEGE.

Principal of the College and all the missionaries to help us, but they say they are already aiding as many as they possibly can. A heathen relative has offered to educate him in India. We do not believe he will become a heathen, even though he studies in a heathen school. We see no other way; we *must* send him to India." We pleaded with them till far into the night. We told them that a man cannot take fire into his bosom and not be burned, and that we had seen the state of things in these heathen schools in India, and felt sure that this boy could not spend four or five years of the most formative period of his life there without being contaminated. However, we could not shake their resolution to send the boy to India.

In imagination we saw the long procession in years to come of just such bright, promising boys going to India and returning lost to purity and to the cause of Christ. We could not bear the thought. We went home that night, got down on our knees and *asked God to help us to raise the funds needed to extend the work of the College. From that hour to this our courage has never faltered—not for a moment. We believe Christ laid the burden of this work on our hearts, and we took it up in the strength of Him who is the great burden-bearer.*

The Board of Directors of the Jaffna College sanctioned our effort. The American Board of Commissioners for Foreign Missions in Boston, whose missionaries we are, kindly granted us permission to come home on furlough, and they have since extended our furlough that we might go on with this work till its completion. We arrived in England on January 1st, 1887. The same year, a committee to aid us in this work was formed in Edinburgh. God has opened many homes and hearts in response, we believe, to the prayers of many in Jaffna who *daily* remember us and this cause before the throne of grace. We have secured up to May, 1890, £17,000, given or promised for the Jaffna College and General Medical Mission. This leaves £13,000 yet to be secured to complete the £30,000 aimed at. However long or however short a time it may take to secure this amount, we intend to continue our efforts, so long as we believe it to be God's will, and so long as He gives us health and a wide open door, until the whole sum is secured.

We would consider several years of work well spent if only we might see the *Jaffna College* permanently equipped with additional foreign and native professorships, with a larger staff of earnest Christian professors and teachers, with scholarships for needy Christian students, with some additional buildings and appliances, and thus enabled better to meet the needs of the people of Jaffna; also a fully-equipped *General Medical Mission* established in connection with it, and under the direction of the same undenominational and unsectarian Board of Directors, to be a blessing to the whole peninsula. We also desire to see, in due time, the establishment of a *Medical Mission for Women.*

We have often been asked if we did not feel anxious as to the success of our scheme. Did we think we should realize our ambition? During the six winters in which we worked among the negroes of the Southern States, before going to Ceylon, and during the seven years we were in Ceylon, if we had one ambition, one aim in life, it was *to do good.* But two years ago, when one of us was ill for two months, and it looked as if perhaps this work, so dear to us, must be given up, we changed our aim in life, and now? Now our *ambition* is *to do the will of God, whatever that may be.* We know *His will is perfect.* We know it is the one utterly good thing in all the world, and that the highest and the only success for us in life consists in doing the will of God day by day.

With regard to the urgent claims of the foreign field, we would like just here to quote a few words from an address of Mr. R. P. Wilder, delivered at a recent meeting in Philadelphia:—

I want to give to you a thought which was suggested to me a few months ago, as I was walking up one of the streets of New York City. The thought was this. I put myself into the places of those people in India; I remembered the story of the Brahman who came to one of our missionaries and said, "Sahib, I have been up North and bathed in the Ranga Nadi to wash away my sins. I have been to shrines in the East and shrines in the West. Once I was young, and now I am old. My hair and beard have grown gray, but I have not found peace. Can you help me?" As I was thinking of that man, my mind went back to the time when Barnabas and Paul crossed the bridge spanning the Orontes. But they go East instead of going West. India is evangelized instead of Greece, China instead of Rome, and Asia instead of Europe, so that the Anglo-Saxon race is left in heathen darkness. It seemed to me that my own father journeyed from one shrine to another trying to find peace. At last he goes to the northern part of the British Isles; and there he sits, under a towering oak, with a Druid priest, trying to find peace. And when he is dying he calls me to his side and says: "Son, once I was young, and now I am old. My hair and my beard have grown gray, but I have not yet found peace. Can you help me?" And I answer, "No, father, I cannot," and he dies. Then I study medicine and astrology, trying to find peace. But one day, in the course of my studies, I meet a man who has seen a missionary. "Oh," he says, "that missionary used wonderful words. He said that 'God so loved the world that He gave His only begotten Son, that whosoever believeth on Him might not perish.'" I stopped him. "Sir," said I, "where can I find that missionary?" He tells me. I start off, and after two weeks' walking, I meet him in a little village in Spain. Again I hear those wonderful words that "God so loved the world that He gave His only begotten Son, that whosoever believeth on Him should not perish, but have everlasting life." "Sir," said I, "how long is it since Christ died?" "Eighteen hundred years." "Your father knew about Christ?" "Yes." "Your grandfather knew about Christ?" "Yes." "Why did not your father come to tell my father? My father spent from childhood to old age seeking peace, and died without it. Sir," said I, "are there many people in your country who know about Christ?" "Yes, we have an average of one minister to every 800 of our population, we have an average of one Christian worker to every forty-eight, and we have an average of one church communicant to every five of our population." "Well, sir," said I, "why don't they come over and tell us Anglo-Saxons about Christ?" He could not answer, and in the still watches of the night, it seemed to me I could hear a voice from on high saying, "*If thou forbear to deliver those that are drawn to death, and those that are ready to be slain, if thou sayest, Behold we knew it not, doth not He that pondereth the heart consider it? And He that keepeth thy soul, doth He not know it? And shall not He render to every man according to his works?*"

Some of the native Christians in Ceylon have made great sacrifices, and endured much persecution and ridicule from their friends and relatives in confessing Christ, and so have proved themselves worthy of the aid which it may cost Christians in this happy and favoured land some little sacrifice to give. The Master says, "Whosoever shall confess Me before men, him will I confess before My Father and before the angels." Is it enough to confess Christ before a small circle of loving friends in one's church at home? Surely it is not for such a small and easy thing that so great a reward is promised. In the early days, confessing Christ meant loss, suffering, martyrdom, if need be Christ asks nothing less of *us* because He asks *everything* of us. "*Whosoever* he be of you that *forsaketh not all that he hath*, he cannot be My disciple." The test of discipleship is the same now as then. Christ asks for entire consecration to Him of all that we are and have. He wants our whole hearts, or none at all, and our time, our talents, and our entire possessions said at His feet, placed at His disposal. The Apostle Paul tells us, "*Ye are not your own, ye are bought with a price.*" Not Paul only, but every Christian should be able to say, "*For me to live is Christ!*"

Livingstone, in Africa, said, "*I will place no value on anything I have or may possess, except in relation to the kingdom of Christ. If anything will advance the interests of that kingdom, it shall be given away or kept only, as, by giving or keeping it, I shall most promote the glory of Him to whom I owe all my hopes in time and in eternity; may grace be given me to adhere to this.*"

If when we read Christ's command and promise, "*Go . . . Lo, I am with you always,*" we could say with Livingstone, "*It is the word of a Gentleman of the most sacred and strictest honour, and there's an end on't,*" surely every service would become a joy, and we could add with that veteran missionary, "*I never made a sacrifice. Can that be called a sacrifice which is simply paid back as a part of a great debt owing to our God, which we can never repay? Is that a sacrifice which brings its own blest reward in healthful activity, the consciousness of doing good, peace of mind, and a bright hope of a glorious destiny hereafter? Away with the word in such a view, and with such a thought! It is emphatically no sacrifice, say rather* IT IS A PRIVILEGE."

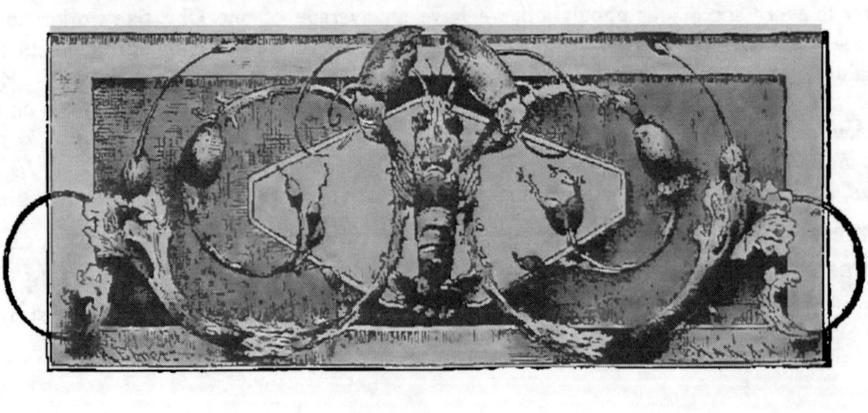

MASK OF A DEVIL-DANCER, OR PROFESSIONAL EXORCIST.

CHAPTER XXXII.

The Medical Mission Agency.

It is our earnest desire to see a General Medical Mission established in North Ceylon, also a Medical Mission for Women, the two working in harmony, and the one being the complement of the other.

Are Medical Missions needed as an *evangelizing* agency in the foreign field? We would like to give, in answer to this question, a few extracts from Dr. Lowe's able book on Medical Missions :—

"The Gospel means 'glad tidings,' and preaching the Gospel means the setting forth of the best of all glad tidings—*the love of God to man.* The heathen, as a rule, can best be taught, as we teach little children in our schools, by object lessons. The Gospel ought, therefore, to be preached to them alike by the living voice and by the unmistakable argument of loving deeds. Like the Apostle Paul, the true missionary, the workman that needeth not to be ashamed, must be able to say, 'By word and deed I have fully preached unto the Gentiles the Gospel of Christ.'

"To the heathen abroad as well as to the godless at home the most convincing proof of the reality and power of the Divine love is that it begets love for man. 'Faith, Hope, Love, these three, but the greatest of these is Love,' love to God begetting love for man; and what is the aim and object of true Christian love? It is the welfare of my brother, the welfare of his body, the welfare of his soul, his welfare for time, his welfare for eternity. Holding forth the Word of Life, both by the living voice and by a practical manifestation of the spirit of the Gospel, is therefore the true meaning of 'Preaching the Gospel.' It implies something more than the mere proclamation of the Gospel message; it implies that, as He who is the sum and substance of the Gospel sympathized with suffering humanity, fed the hungry, healed the sick, and went about continually doing good, thus ever manifesting the spirit of His own religion, and teaching by His 'gracious words,' and by His loving deeds, its principles, so His ambassadors must 'preach the Gospel,' not by word only, but likewise by a loving, benevolent, Christ-like ministry performed in Christ's name and for His sake.

"The evangelization of the world is Christ's own work, and those who, as His instruments, are called to engage in it, are commissioned to represent Christ, to represent Him in His tender pity for the lost, in His loving sympathy for the afflicted, in His care for the sick and His compassion for the suffering. We turn, therefore, to Christ's ministry on earth for the interpretation of His own commission, 'Go ye into all the world and preach the Gospel to every creature.'

"In reading the New Testament one cannot fail to be struck with the fact that our Lord's personal ministry on earth as well as that of His Apostles was pre-eminently that of the medical missionary. In the last three verses of the fourth chapter of St. Matthew's Gospel we read: 'And Jesus went about all Galilee, teaching in their synagogues, and preaching the gospel of the kingdom, and healing all manner of sickness and all manner of disease among the people. And His fame went throughout all Syria: and they brought unto Him all sick people that were taken with divers diseases and torments, and those which were lunatic, and those that had the palsy; and He healed them. And there followed Him great multitudes of people from Galilee, and from Decapolis, and from Jerusalem, and from Judea, and from beyond Jordan.'

"Our Lord was just then entering upon His public ministry. He knew man's heart, the way to gain access to it, its prejudices, and the many obstacles in the way of the people receiving His teaching; and knowing all this, such were the means He employed to reveal His character and claims, to remove prejudice, and to draw men nearer to Himself. By the exercise of His healing power He gathered around Him a great congregation, with hearts overflowing with gratitude, and thus the searching truths of 'The Sermon on the Mount' fell as living seed on a prepared soil. When we inquire into our Lord's recorded miracles, we find that *no fewer than two-thirds were miracles of healing*. . . . These miraculous works of healing were unanswerable proofs that He was what He claimed to be, the Son of God; but they were more, they were living manifestations of the spirit of His own religion; they spoke a language intelligible to every human conscience; they revealed His tender compassion, His loving sympathy, His incomprehensible love, and in this light His own disciples regarded them as the fulfilment of the word of Esaias, 'Himself took our infirmities, and bare our sicknesses.'

"As the Divine Author and Founder of Christianity, the record of our Lord's personal ministry must ever be to us deeply suggestive and instructive. Every feature of that ministry claims our devout attention. His mode of commending the truth in so far as it was supernatural, we cannot imitate, but in so far as the outcome of His 'mighty works' was meant to be a manifestation of the spirit of the Gospel (as much needed now as then) 'He hath left us an example that we should follow in His steps.'

"As our authority for the employment of this agency we have not only our Lord's example, but likewise His direct command. What He did Himself He commissioned His Apostles and the first teachers of Christianity to do likewise: 'And into whatsoever city ye enter . . . heal the sick that are therein, and say unto them, The Kingdom of God is come nigh unto you.' . . . It may be said, however, that it was by the forth-putting of His own Divine power that Christ did these 'mighty works,' which spread His fame throughout all Syria, and that it was in virtue of their miraculous endowments (now no longer available) that His disciples made the deaf to hear, the blind to see, and the lame to walk, and that, therefore, their method cannot now be a model for our imitation. Such an inference would be legitimate were these miracles intended merely as attestations to the Divinity of Christ, and as proofs of the Divine origin of the Gospel which the disciples were commissioned to proclaim; but, as we have already seen, they were more than this—they were a practical manifestation of the compassionate spirit of Christ's religion; they spoke in a language that could not be misunderstood, of Him who came, 'Not to destroy men's lives, but to save them.' And surely, in so far as this was the Divine intention, these miracles of healing are recorded for our instruction, teaching us that, in our missionary enterprises, the consecration of the healing art to the service of the Gospel is not only in accordance with the Divine method, but forms a part of the Divine intention.

"The 'gift of tongues,' which enabled these first heralds of the Cross to proclaim to

men of all nations 'the wonderful works of God,' is not now miraculously bestowed, neither is the 'gift of healing;' but in the one case as in the other, the qualification which the 'gift' conveyed must be patiently and laboriously acquired. 'He sent them to preach the Kingdom of God, and to heal the sick.'

"The Church recognizes the Divine commission to 'preach the Gospel to every creature' as still binding upon her, notwithstanding the withdrawal of the 'gift of tongues.' Shall the command of our Lord in reference to 'healing the sick,' which formed so prominent a feature of His own earthly ministry and that of His Apostles, be ignored on the ground that miraculous 'gifts of healing' are now withheld? Nay, rather, the withdrawal of those gifts renders it all the more imperative that we should cultivate and consecrate, with the utmost energy and devotion, not only the science of philology, but likewise that of medicine, that so we may fulfil our Lord's commission in all its breadth and fulness, and following His example, preach the Gospel 'by word and deed.'"

Missionaries of three societies have been at work in the northern province of Ceylon for over seventy years. At the present time there are less than 3000 Christian communicants in the province. *If the remaining* 313,000 *are to be won to Christ in this generation*, and surely nothing less than this should be our aim and effort, it seems very desirable that an *additional agency*, and especially the agency of *Medical Missions*, should be introduced. As the large numbers of heathen doctors are the strongest allies of the heathen priests in Jaffna, so a Medical Mission in Jaffna would be the strongest ally of all the Christian agencies now at work. How can Jaffna become largely Christian so long as the majority of the people in times of sickness resort to heathen doctors, and make vows and offerings to heathen gods? Heathenism is still so gross and rampant in North Ceylon, that mission agencies can hardly count the battle there to be much more than begun.

We need *Medical Missionaries* who will go to the people in their times of sorrow and anxiety, and by giving them actual relief, win their gratitude and affection, and by showing them the very spirit of Christ, gain the assent of *their hearts* to Him. The Medical Missionary comes nearer to the people in loving ministry than the average missionary who has no medical knowledge. In the two months of December, 1888, and January, 1889, abont 2000 people died in Jaffna from an epidemic of fever, among whom very few had received proper treatment. When smallpox, cholera, or epidemics of malignant fever break out from time to time, the people die by thousands. Forty native communicants died in Jaffna last year. To have saved the lives of some of these trained and experienced workers would have been of incalculable value to the cause. Of course, as a Christian man, the Medical Missionary will strive to improve every opportunity of doing personal work among his patients in the hospital and dispensary, and at their own homes.

His Excellency Sir Arthur Gordon, K.C.B., when visiting Jaffna, strongly urged that a medical work similar to that done formerly by Dr. Green should be resumed, and followed up his suggestion by heading the list with a subscription of Rs. 1000 for this object. W. C. Twynam, Esq., for something like thirty years Government Agent in Ceylon, and an able, far-sighted, and public-spirited man, has also strongly urged that a Medical Mission should be established. The work the Medical Missionary is to conduct will be under the direction of a Board composed of missionaries and native Christians of the Church of England, Wesleyan, and American Missions, the three missionary societies carrying on work in Jaffna. This Board of Directors are also the Directors of the Jaffna College.

John Henry Marston, M.R.C.S., L.R.C.P., formerly connected with the Mildmay Mission in London, has been appointed by the Board of Directors to take charge of the General Medical Mission in North Ceylon, and he has gone out with his wife to undertake this work.

We would earnestly commend Dr. and Mrs. Marston to the affectionate and prayerful remembrance of all who love the Master and desire to see His Kingdom come in Ceylon. Dr. Marston is the only *Missionary Physician* in the Northern Province among 316,000 people, and, with the exception of the civil surgeon, the only fully qualified medical man, we believe, in the province.

A Medical Mission Hospital is the *strategic* point in the *evangelistic work* of a Medical Mission. It is from the *Mission Hospital* that the majority of converts are found to come, in the experience of the most successful Medical Missions on record. It is in the *Mission Hospital* that the patient comes to know the missionary and his assistants, to see exemplified in their daily lives the spirit and power of

The water in which the feet of a fakir is washed is given to the sick to be drunk as a medicine.

A FAKIR.

the Gospel. It is there that he learns, little by little, to believe the truth which he hears read and sung and spoken from day to day, and to reveal his doubts and difficulties, and have them removed.

DR. J. H. MARSTON.

On this point, Dr. Lowe says in his book on Medical Missions: "It is in the hospital that the most satisfactory and successful medical and surgical work will be accomplished—work which will produce the deepest impressions, and direct public attention most favourably to the higher objects of the mission. It is here, too, that the Medical Missionary will be able most successfully to accomplish evangelistic work—here that he may expect to gather the most precious and enduring fruit. While dispensary work and occasionally medico-evangelistic tours among the surrounding towns and villages are important features of Medical Mission work, still the hospital will be the field in which the richest harvest will be reaped, and therefore the establishment of a hospital should from the first be kept in view, and accomplished at the earliest opportunity." Sums sufficient for the erection of a Medical Mission Hospital in Jaffna have been given or promised.

One hundred pounds will endow a bed in the hospital (providing permanently for a part of the expense of its up-keep) ; £50 will provide the half, and £25 the quarter of the endowment of a bed ; £10 will provide a share in a bed.*

Are there not some friends in Great Britain and America who could each contribute one of the above-named sums, without diminishing their ordinary subscriptions to other Christian objects, and thus have a real part in this much-needed Christ-like medical work in Ceylon?

* This will provide for the patients the shelter and ordinary comforts of the hospital, and the attendance of the missionary physician, free of charge, leaving them to meet the cost of medicine, food, and incidentals, which expenses they would have had to bear had they remained in their own homes.

TWO DEVIL-DANCERS.

Three kind friends have of late greatly encouraged us by donations of £100 each. One of these, J. Campbell White, Esq., who gave £100 at the beginning of our effort for a scholarship in the Jaffna College, has kindly given £100 for the General Medical Mission, saying that, as he had helped us to secure *the first half* of the fund which we were seeking, he would give us a similar help towards the *last half.* Are there not others among the friends who have helped us in securing the first half of the fund who will follow his example, and give a *second donation* towards the last half of the fund?

It would add to the interest of the effort if the donors were to associate with their gifts their name, or the name of some one whom they have honoured and loved, and if these names were engraved on brass tablets, which would be permanently connected with the beds thus endowed, this would give a personality to the gift in the eyes of the people of Jaffna, and would lead them to feel that Christians in distant lands had loved them, and made sacrifices on their behalf, and were entitled to their gratitude in return.

We will most gladly pledge £100 in memory of our beloved parents. Cannot others be found who will do the same in remembrance of those dear to them, and for the sake of a work which has as its great object to promote the progress of the Redeemer's kingdom? The members of some family circles, and perhaps of some congregations, Sabbath-schools, Bible-classes, Y.M.C.A.'s, Y.W.C.A.'s, &c., might unite their gifts to present such a tribute to the memory of a parent, a pastor, a teacher, a president, or a friend, who has gone to be with Jesus. Would it be a less acceptable monument than a memorial window or a costly tomb? A short time ago, in response to our appeal, the students of the Old Hall, Wellington, pledged not merely a donation of £100, but £100 *annually* to support a medical lady under the I.F.N.S. and I. Society as *their own missionary* in Benares. Might not the example of liberality set by the students in this school be followed by many others? Sums promised for beds might be paid in *instalments during five years* if the givers or collectors so desired.

We earnestly hope that there may be many who will thus provide a thank-offering to God, a permanent aid to the Medical Mission in Ceylon, and a grateful memorial of friends whose work on earth is finished. Surely God will plead the cause of the oppressed, and there are thousands upon thousands in North Ceylon oppressed by in and superstition, and held down by heathen priests and doctors. Surely the cause which seeks to deliver their bodies from needless suffering, and their minds and hearts from the powers of darkness and evil, must be the cause of humanity and of Christ.

Feeling the great and pressing need of a Medical Mission for Women in North Ceylon, and believing that it was God's will that such a work should be begun, since He had led kind friends, entirely unasked by us, to promise the salary of a lady doctor, and other friends to promise and give additional sums, we were led to present the matter to the Committee of the I.F.N.S. and I. Society. We offered to transfer to that Society all pledges and sums already given for the object, and to do all in our power as occasion arose to secure for them the remainder of the amount needed to organize and sustain such a work, viz. £3000 for the erection of a Medical Mission-house and a Women's and Children's Hospital, and £450 in annual subscriptions toward the up-keep of the hospital and dispensary, and the support of the European and native workers, provided the Society would inaugurate the work as their own, and take it under their entire control.

MOTHER AND CHILD.

To our great joy, on the 19th of last June, the Committee of the I.F.N.S. and I. Society, in the most cordial manner, acceded to our request that they should establish a medical work for women in North Ceylon, having in contemplation a hospital for women and children, a mission-house, two fully qualified lady doctors, with a staff of native assistants, the work to be undertaken at the earliest date possible. We thank God for this token of His favour, and take new courage to go on with the effort. This Medical Mission for Women and also the General Medical Mission will both be located in North Ceylon Each of these missions will have its separate and distinct work, a work which it only can do, and both, we trust, will co-operate to the fullest extent with every other agency already employed in the great work of evangelizing the people and bringing them to the knowledge and service of Christ. These two Medical Missions, working side by

LOW CASTE WOMEN, SUCH AS ARE NOW COMMONLY EMPLOYED AS NURSES TO THE SICK.

side and in fullest harmony, will each strengthen the work of the other. According to God's arithmetic, two are worth not merely twice as many as one, but ten times as many. "How should one chase a thousand, and two put ten thousand to flight?" (Deut. xxxii. 30.)

We wish to quote here the words of Professor Miller, in an address at one of the annual meetings of the Edinburgh Medical Missionary Society. He said :—

"When we come before you with Scripture warrant on our side—with the personal example of our Lord and His Apostles not only beckoning us on, but reproving us for not having come—with the successful experience of medical missions, as far as they have yet been tried, speaking strongly in our favour, and with the united and cordial approval of every missionary with whom we have ever come in contact; when missionaries all tell us that they find the medical element so essential to the success of their work that they are compelled sometimes to practise it themselves; when labourers from all quarters of the mission-field, men gallantly bearing the burden and heat of the day, are calling to us anxiously for medical colleagues, not on account of their own health, but to assist them in their great work of reaching the hearts of men whose souls they seek to save; and when, had we but the means and men, we might now plant, not one or two or three, but many Medical Missions in the very heart and strongholds of heathenism, where they would be gladly welcomed, and by-and-by supported to a considerable extent by the very heathen themselves; with such claims as these, surely it is neither unbecoming nor unwarrantable that we ask earnestly and importunately for your sympathy and aid. And bear with me, if I remind you that you have an important duty to discharge towards the medical profession, that you owe it a debt. Is there any one here who does not feel and acknowledge that debt? Has no father, or brother, or sister, or husband, or wife, or child, been saved to you, under God's providence, by the skill and care of the physician? At a time when all seemed dark and hopeless, and you dared not look into the future, at a time when the blackness of despair had settled down, and well-nigh shut out heaven from your sight and prayer from your lips, at a time when you would gladly have given all the earthly treasure you possessed, or ever might possess, in barter for the life which seemed so fast and hopelessly ebbing away, has not the physician then seemed to you as a ministering angel sent to comfort you? Have you not then clung to him as your best earthly friend, your only earthly hope and stay? And when success attended his efforts in battling with disease and death, when life, and hope, and health came smiling back, have you not wet his hand with your tears of gratitude, and sent him away laden with your blessing and your prayers? Or was it your own life that was quivering in the balance at a time, perhaps, when a downward turn would have hazarded a double death, but when the upward cast, still due, apparently, to the hand of the physician, bade you live again for time and for eternity? Ah, then surely the argument we now venture to use will come home with a double force. Each one who has felt this, or aught like this, will surely acknowledge a large and growing debt of obligation. Let those debts be all accumulated into one vast whole, not due, or at least not to be rendered to the individual man, but to the God-like profession which they represent. The opportunity is given you to discharge in some measure that debt now.

"Honours, in old times, were freely accorded to individual practitioners of renown; medals were struck in their honour, bearing the legend 'ob cives servatos' (on account of citizens preserved). We seek no such personal gifts, but we ask you to honour the profession by helping it to honour and adorn itself, by helping it to write on the bells of the horses 'Holiness unto the Lord,' by helping it to be instrumental in saving the souls as well as the bodies of men, by helping it to place in its coronet new jewels of greatest value and of brightest lustre, by helping it to twine in its garland a new wreath from the ever-green and ever-growing plant of renown. And let me add that, in thus honouring the profession, you will honour also that profession's Head. Medicine has been at no time without her gods. The early Greeks owned Apollo; after him came Æsculapius; and gods and demigods followed in abundance. But the power of advancing civilization struck away those unsightly capitals from the otherwise goodly column; not to leave it mutilated and bare, but to make way for the true headstone, to exalt and acknowledge the great Physician, Jehovah Rophi, the Lord the healer—no mythical personage, but He who in very deed dwelt with men upon the earth, who went about continually doing good, and who has promised to be with His faithful followers alway, even unto the end of the world.

"Such is the double debt and double duty which we ask you now in part, at least, to discharge. But do not mistake the nature of the claim which we make. We seek your pecuniary aid to carry on this great and noble enterprise so beneficent to men, so glorifying to God; but we do not want your money only. 'Your money or your life' is the startling demand of the highwayman; ours is more startling still—'Your money and your life.' Of some select, gifted, and gallant few, we seek their lives, wholly devoted to the death if need be, in the service of their great Master. But of all, we seek their life in one sense, in the sense of claiming that on which true life depends, that whereby spiritual life is fed and maintained, without which it dies, prayer—intercession at the Throne of Grace! . . . And if it be true that the deadly conflict is now at hand between truth and error, between the powers of light and the powers of darkness, if the time is now near when we shall be involved as combatants for very life in that eventful struggle, how can we look for Heaven's aid, how dare we ask it, unless we be on Heaven's side, and doing the will of Him who sits almighty there? How can we, in the shock of the coming battle, and in the turmoil of the approaching fray, be otherwise than helpless and overborne, unless, as faithful soldiers of the Cross, we be found mustered around and fighting under the banner of the Captain of the hosts of the Lord, following where that banner leads, losing neither sight nor hold of it—the banner of Him, whose latest command it was, whose very watchword of the fight is, 'Go ye unto all the world, and preach the Gospel to every creature.'

"'And He sent them to preach the Kingdom of God, and to heal the sick . . . And they departed, and went through the towns, preaching the Gospel and healing everywhere.'" (Luke ix. 2-6.)

A company of devil-dancers.

WHA'S MY NEIBOR?

BY GEORGE MACDONALD, LL.D.

DOON frae Jerus'lem a traveller tuik The laigh road to Jericho ;
It had an ill name an' mony a cruik, It was lang an' unco how.

Oot cam' the robbers an' fell on the man, An' knockit him on
the heid ;
Took a' whauron they could lay their han', And left him nakit
for deid.

By cam' a minister o' the kirk : "A sair mishanter !" he cried ;
"Wha kens whaur the villains may lurk ? I's haud to the ither side.'

By cam' an elder o' the kirk ; Like a young horse *he* shied ;
"Fie ! there's a bonny mornin's wark !" An' he spang't to the ither side.

By cam' ane gaed to the wrang kirk, Douce he trotted alang ;
"Puir body !" he cried, an' wi' a yerk, Aff o' his cuddy he sprang ;

He ran to the body an' turn'd it ower, "There's life i' the man !" he cried ;
He wasna ane to stan' an' glower, An' haud to the ither side.

He doctor'd his wounds an' heised him on To the back of the beasty douce ;
An' held him there, till, a weary man, He langt at the half-way house.

He ten'd him a' nicht, an' at dawn o' day, "Lan'lord" (he says) "latna him lack ;
There's auchteenpence ; ony mair ootlay I'll sattle as I come back."

Sae nae mair, neibors—say nae sic word, Wi' hert aye arguin' an' chill ;
No, "Whae's the neibor to me, O Lord ?" But, "Wha am I neibor till ?"

BANYAN AND COCOANUT TREES IN CEYLON.

NATIVE BIBLE READER.

APPENDIX.

THE story of Maria Peabody, from the pen of some unknown friend, appeared in *Life and Light.* It is true in all its details, and we append it here in the hope that it may encourage those who cannot *go* to the foreign field in person to *give* in aid of the work. Ought not every man and every woman, who can do so, to support a *representative* as *their personal substitute* among the heathen?

Mrs. Grattan Guinness has said, "*We have no fires of martyrdom now to test our fidelity to Jesus Christ; but we are not left without a test. God is testing us all continually as to the measure of our* FAITH, LOVE, AND DEVOTEDNESS TO HIS SON *by the presence of* ONE THOUSAND MILLIONS OF HEATHEN IN THE WORLD. *It is a tremendous test; so real, so practical! Gifts that cost us no personal self-denial are no proof of devotedness.*"

THE STORY OF MARIA PEABODY.

"Of a truth I say unto you, that this . . . hath cast in more than they all; for all these have of their abundance cast in unto the offerings of God; but she of her penury hath cast in all . . . that she had."—*St. Luke* xxi. 3, 4.

IN the beautiful island of *Ceylon*, many years ago, the native Christians, who had long worshipped in bungalows and old Dutch chapels, decided that they must have a church built for themselves. Enthusiastic givers were each eager to forward the new enterprise. But to the amazement of all, *Maria Peabody*, a lone orphan girl, who had been a beneficiary in the girls' schools at *Oodooville*, came forward and offered to give the land upon which to build, which was the best site in her native village.

Not only was it all she owned in this world, but, far more, it was her marriage portion, and in making this gift, in the eyes of every native, she renounced all hopes of being married. As this alternative in the East was regarded as an awful step, many thought her beside herself, and tried to dissuade her from such an act of renunciation. "No," said *Maria;* "I have given it to Jesus, and as He has accepted it, you must." And so to-day the first Christian church in *Ceylon* (the first chapel built by natives) stands upon land given by a poor orphan girl.

The deed was noised abroad, and came to the knowledge of a young theological student, who was also a beneficiary of the mission, and it touched his heart. Neither could he rest, until he had sought and won the rare and noble maiden who was willing to give up so much in her Master's cause.*

Some one in the United States had been for years contributing twenty dollars annually for the support of this young Hindu girl, but the donor was unknown. The Rev. Dr. Poor, a missionary in *Ceylon*, visiting *America* about that time, longed to ascertain who was the faithful sower, and report the wonderful harvest. Finding himself in *Hanover*, *N.H.*, preaching to the students at *Dartmouth College*, he happened in conversation to hear some one speak of *Mrs. Peabody*, and repeated, "*Peabody; what Peabody?*" "*Mrs. Maria Peabody*, who resides here—the widow of a former professor," was the answer. "Oh! I must see her before I leave," said the earnest man, about to continue his journey. The first words after an introduction at her house, were: "I have come to bring you a glad report; for I cannot but think that it is to you we in *Ceylon* owe the opportunity of educating one who has proved as lovely and consistent a native convert as we have ever had. She is exceptionally interesting, devotedly pious, and bears your name."

"Alas!" said the lady, "although the girl bears my name, I wish I could claim the honour of educating her; it belongs not to me, but to *Louisa Osborne*, my poor coloured cook. Some years ago in *Salem*, *Mass.*, she came to me after an evening meeting, saying: 'I have just heard that if anybody would give twenty dollars a year, they could support and educate a child in *Ceylon*, and I have decided to do it. They say that along with the money I can send a name: and I have come, mistress, to ask you if you would object to my sending yours.' "At that time," continued the lady, "a servant's wages ranged from a dollar to a dollar and a half a week, yet my cook had for a long time been contributing half a dollar each month at the monthly concert for foreign missions. There were those who expostulated with her for giving away so much for one in her circumstances, as a time might come when she could not earn. 'I have thought it all over,' she would reply, 'and concluded I would rather give what I can while I am earning, and then if I lose my health and cannot work, why, there is the poor-house, and I can go there. You see they have no poor-house in heathen lands, for it is only Christians who care for the poor.'" In telling this story. Dr. Poor used to pause at this point, and exclaim: "To the poor-house! Do you

* This young man, after completing his theological studies, was stationed, with his wife, in a district called Alavertty. At that time nearly all the people in that district were idolaters. Now in that district there is a church with forty members, an inquirer's class, a large Sabbath school, and five or six village day-schools with several hundreds of children in attendance, to whom the Bible lessons are regularly taught. This change, through God's blessing, has largely resulted from the efforts of these two consecrated Christians.

N

believe God would ever let that good woman die in the poor-house? Never!" We shall see.

The missionary learned that the last known of *Louisa Osborne* was that she was residing in *Lowell, Mass.* In due time his duties called him to that city. At the close of an evening service before a crowded house, he related among missionary incidents, as a crowning triumph, the story of *Louisa Osborne* and *Maria Peabody.* The disinterested devotion, self-sacrifice, and implicit faith and zeal of the Christian giver in favoured *America* has been developed, matured, and well-nigh eclipsed, by her faithful *protégée* in far-off benighted *India* His heart glowing with zeal, and deeply stirred by the fresh retrospect of the triumphs of the Gospel over heathenism, he exclaimed, "If there is any one present who knows anything of that good woman, *Louisa Osborne*, and will lead me to her, I shall be greatly obliged." The benediction pronounced and the crowd dispersing, Dr. Poor passed down one of the aisles, chatting with the pastor, when he espied a quiet little figure apparently waiting for him. Could it be her? Yes, it was a coloured woman, and it must be *Louisa Osborne*. With quickened steps he reached her, exclaiming in tones of suppressed emotion, "I believe this is my sister in Christ, *Louisa Osborne?*" "That is my name," was the calm reply. "Well, God bless you, *Louisa*; you have heard my report, and know all; but before we part, probably never to meet again in this world, I want you to answer me one question. What made you do it?" With downcast eyes, and in a low and trembling voice, she replied, "Well, I do not know, but I guess it was my Lord Jesus."

They parted only to meet in the streets of the *New Jerusalem*; for the missionary returned to his adopted home, where, ere long, the loving hands of his faithful native brethren bore him to his honoured grave. The humble handmaiden of the Lord laboured meekly on a while, and is ending her failing days, not in a poorhouse, verily, but, through the efforts of those who knew her best, in a pleasant, comfortable Old Ladies' Home. "Him that honoureth Me, I will honour."

The seal of *Calvin*, one of the great apostles of the Reformation, represents a hand holding a burning heart, illustrative of his life-principle: "I give thee all; I keep back nothing for myself." Centuries afterward, two humble followers of the Master caught a kindred inspiration from the same divine source. Shall we, to whom so much of privilege and bounty is granted, lay down this marvellous story of self-renunciation, and let its lesson be lost on our own lives?

"Unto whomsoever much is given, of him shall be much required." (Luke xii. 48.)

Remittances for the College or Medical Mission may be sent to C. H. WARNER, Treasurer, Bank of Commerce, Boston, Mass.

Form of Bequest.

I bequeath to the JAFFNA COLLEGE, Ceylon, the sum of $ ...., free of duty, to be paid out of that part of my personal Estate which by law may be effectually given for the benefit of the said JAFFNA COLLEGE,* and for which sum the receipt of the Treasurer for the time being shall be a sufficient discharge.*

[THREE WITNESSES.]

*If it is desired that the Legacy be applied toward the *General Medical Mission in connection with the Jaffna College*, these words should be used in place of "Jaffna College."

THE JAFFNA COLLEGE,

AND

GENERAL MEDICAL MISSION IN NORTH CEYLON.

Referees in Great Britain.

The Rt. Hon. the EARL OF ABERDEEN.
The Rt. Hon. the LORD KINNAIRD.
The Rt. Hon. the LORD POLWARTH.
EDWARD CROSSLEY, Esq., M.P.
Rev. H. GRATTAN GUINNESS, F.R.G.S.
J. E. MATHIESON, Esq.
J. L. MAXWELL, Esq., M.D.
W. T. PATON Esq.
Rev. NEVILL SHERBROOKE.
Rev. FRANK WHITE
J. CAMPBELL WHITE, Esq.
GEORGE WILLIAMS, Esq.
The DOWAGER COUNTESS CAIRNS.
Lady VICTORIA BUXTON.
Mrs. H. GRATTAN GUINNESS.
Mrs. STEPHEN MENZIES.

Edinburgh Auxiliary Committee.

Chairman—Sir WILLIAM MUIR, K.C S.I., LL.D., D C.L.
Honorary Secretary and Treasurer—GEORGE C. MACLEAN, Esq., 4, Dean Park Crescent, Edinburgh.

Rev. ARMSTRONG BLACK.
Rev. HENRY DUNCAN.
Rev. CHARLES R. TEAPE, Ph.D.
Rev ANDREW THOMSON, D D.
Rev. ALEXANDER WHYTE, D.D.
Rev. GEORGE WILSON.
ROBERT SIMSON, Esq., H.M.B C.S.
J. DUNCAN SMITH, E-q., S.S.C.
Major-General F. NEPEAN SMITH
Mrs. DUNCAN.
Miss HUNTER.
Miss MACKENZIE.
Mrs. MACRAE.
Mrs. MILLAR.
Mrs. SIMSON.
Mrs. SMITH.
Mrs. STUART.
Mrs. WHITSON.

Honorary Collectors.

The Misses M. and M. W. LEITCH, c/o S. Stanton, Esq., 17, Southampton Row, London, W.C.

Bankers.

Messrs. BARCLAY, BEVAN, TRITTON, RANSOM, BOUVERIE & Co., 1, Pall Mall East, London.
The BANK OF SCOTLAND, Edinburgh.

Auditors.

ARTHUR J. HILL, VELLACOTT & Co., Chartered Accountants, 1, Finsbury Circus, London, E.C.

My Refuge.

"In the secret of Thy presence."—*Psalm* 31: 20.

The following Verses were written by ELLEN LAKSHIM GOREH, a Brahmin Lady of the highest caste.

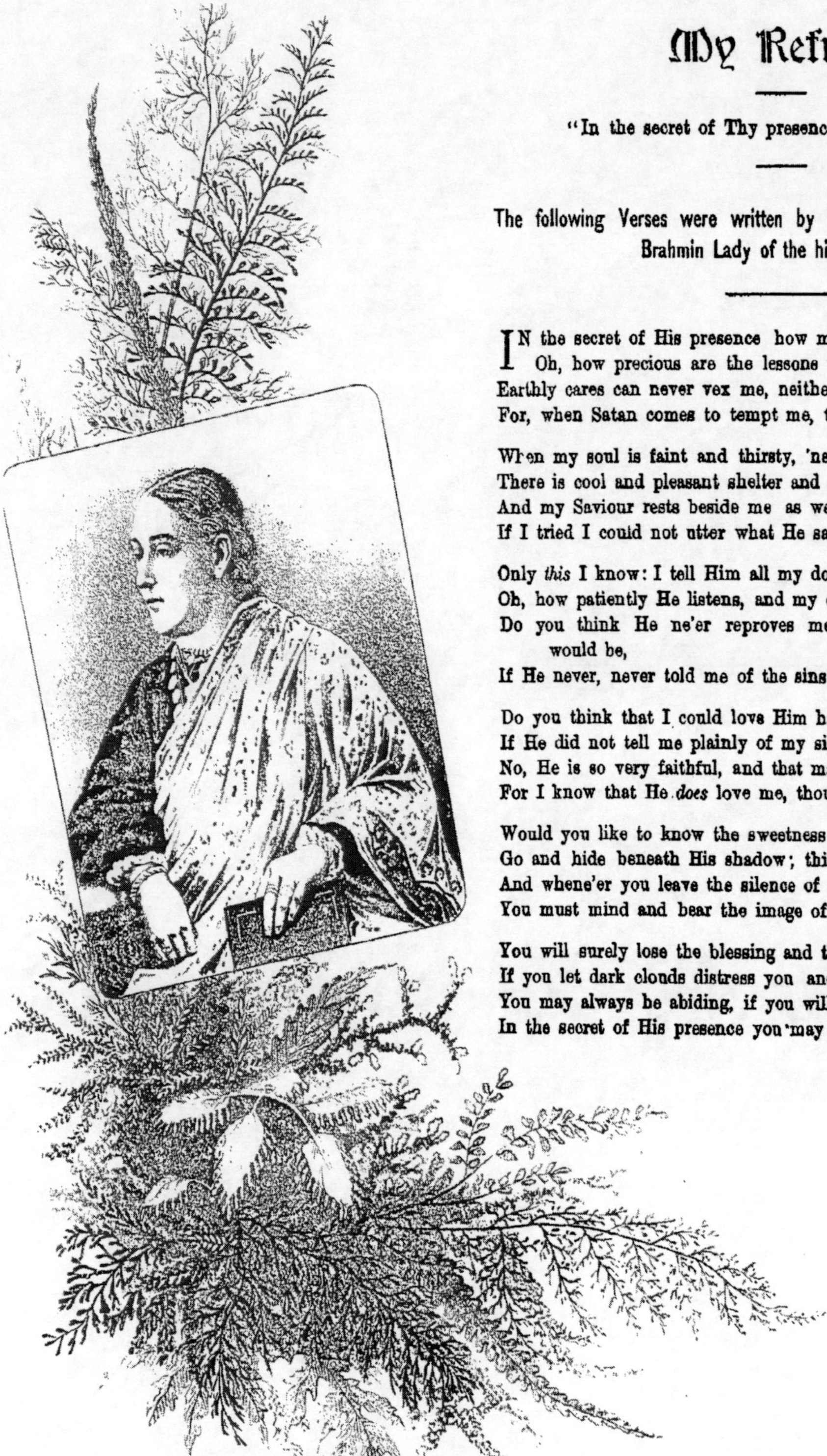

IN the secret of His presence how my soul delights to hide!
  Oh, how precious are the lessons which I learn at Jesus' side!
Earthly cares can never vex me, neither trials lay me low,
For, when Satan comes to tempt me, to the secret place I go.

When my soul is faint and thirsty, 'neath the shadow of His wing
There is cool and pleasant shelter and a fresh and crystal spring;
And my Saviour rests beside me as we hold communion sweet:
If I tried I could not utter what He says when thus we meet.

Only *this* I know: I tell Him all my doubts and griefs and fears;
Oh, how patiently He listens, and my drooping soul He cheers!
Do you think He ne'er reproves me? What a false friend He
  would be,
If He never, never told me of the sins which he must see!

Do you think that I could love Him half so well, or as I ought,
If He did not tell me plainly of my sinful deed and thought?
No, He is so very faithful, and that makes me trust him more,
For I know that He *does* love me, though he wounds me very sore.

Would you like to know the sweetness of the secret of the Lord?
Go and hide beneath His shadow; this shall then be your reward.
And whene'er you leave the silence of the special meeting place,
You must mind and bear the image of your Master in your face.

You will surely lose the blessing and the fulness of your joy,
If you let dark clouds distress you and your inward peace destroy.
You may always be abiding, if you will, at Jesus' side,
In the secret of His presence you may every moment hide.